MORNING GLORIES

MORNING GLORIES
DONNA LEAHY
FOOD PHOTOGRAPHY BY
JERRY ORABONA
SCENIC PHOTOGRAPHY BY
ROBERT F. LEAHY
RIZZOLI
NEW YORK

Photo, preceding pages: *Cinnamon French Toast with Apricot-Cheese Filling; Pineapple with Blackberries, Figs and Lemon*

First published in the United States of America in 1996 by
Rizzoli International Publications, Inc.
300 Park Avenue South
New York, NY 10010

Library of Congress Cataloging–in–Publication Data
Leahy, Donna.
Morning Glories : recipes for breakfast, brunch, and beyond from an American country inn / Donna Leahy.
p. cm.
Includes index.
ISBN 0-8478-1923-X (hc)
1. Breakfasts. 2. Brunches. 3. Inn at Twin Linden (Churchtown, Pa.)
I. Title.
TX733.L43 1996
641.5'2—dc20 95-49832
CIP

Designed by Joel Avirom
Design Assistant: Jason Snyder

Printed and bound in Singapore

Dedicated to my favorite photographer, partner and friend.

With special thanks to Dan Green and Carole Lalli for their enthusiasm, support and expertise; to Joel Avirom for his artistic eye and for the funny story about two New Yorkers at a self-service gas station; to photographers Jerry Orabona and Bob Leahy (OK Jerry, you can be my *second* favorite photographer); to my family for loving me and for never saying I'm crazy, despite what they might think from time to time; to Mom for letting me stir the batter and to Roseanne for being the quintessential big sister; to my friend Gail Kent for showing us what a first-rate inn is supposed to be; to our Plain farmers and neighbors for their dedication to quality; and to our loyal guests and fellow lovers of food, especially those who keep asking, "When's Donna's cookbook coming out?"

CONTENTS

100
Toot horn
for Service

INTRODUCTION

BREAKFAST—THE FORGOTTEN MEAL

In the world of haute cuisine, breakfast is the forgotten meal. Think of it. What was the last interesting dish you can recall being served for breakfast? And why does it always seem so easy to skip what is so often called by nutritionists "the most important meal of the day?" The answer is simple: most breakfasts are boring. Even the food magazines can't seem to get around it. While other menus entice us with their culinary ingenuity and beautiful presentations, the rare breakfast feature invariably includes the same old familiar items served in the same old family-style way. Rarer still and perhaps nonexistent is the feature about a world-famous chef preparing breakfast. Our breakfast involves a great amount of planning by the same chef who prepares our elaborate dinners. I am that person. I don't know of any other fine restaurant or five-star hotel that can make this claim. If you think you don't like breakfast, this book is your invitation to forever change the way you look at it—by offering you a whole new cuisine given the same care and attention as the finest dinner. If you already love breakfast, get ready to challenge your palate and eye with new and exciting dishes, not merely remakes of the old breakfast standards.

I've made an unofficial survey while clearing empty breakfast dishes at our inn. Often I am told, "I don't usually eat breakfast, but I just couldn't help but finish everything." Our guests, who might be considered "foodies," actually choose our inn because of the breakfast. Describing breakfast with the word "gourmet" in its original sense may not seem appropriate, but our morning meals incorporate the unique creativity associated with gourmet cuisine. The creativity that brings out the subtleties of food seldom is applied with enthusiasm to the morning meal. What sets our breakfast cuisine apart is its refined approach, incorporating a careful balance of health, taste and presentation—the same qualities that make for a fabulous "gourmet" dinner.

Because breakfast is an integral part of the overall culinary experience of our inn, our unique menu selections must go far beyond Eggs Benedict. And because a good part of our clientele consists of returning guests, my breakfast ideas must always be fresh and innovative. Some recipes require little preplanning, whereas others are more complicated. The bonus is that often much of the preparation can be done a day or two in advance. Impractical? Not really, when you consider the time you might invest preparing a formal dinner or even a picnic lunch. Of course, these are special meals and may not be appropriate on an everyday basis—but how many "gourmet" dinners do you prepare on weeknights? And is there any meal at once so civilized and luxurious as a wonderful breakfast served in bed on a leisurely morning?

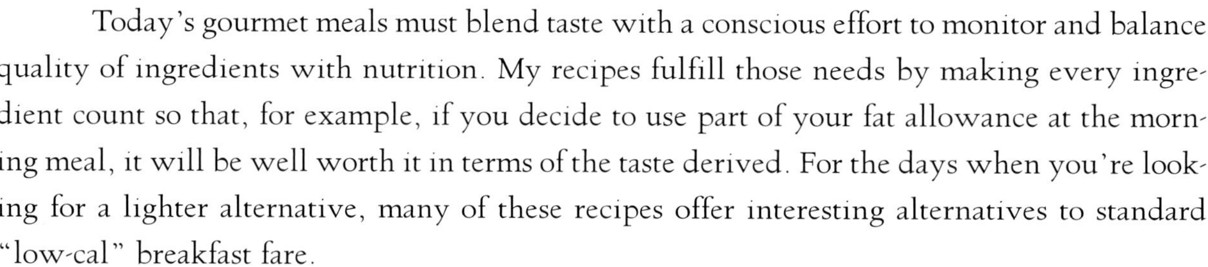

Today's gourmet meals must blend taste with a conscious effort to monitor and balance quality of ingredients with nutrition. My recipes fulfill those needs by making every ingredient count so that, for example, if you decide to use part of your fat allowance at the morning meal, it will be well worth it in terms of the taste derived. For the days when you're looking for a lighter alternative, many of these recipes offer interesting alternatives to standard "low-cal" breakfast fare.

Since our hurried lives don't always afford us the opportunity to get away when we need to, an elegant morning meal can supply the needed break without leaving home. And how pleasantly surprised your friends and colleagues might be to receive an invitation to an exquisite breakfast or brunch rather than the same old dinner party offerings. Whether at an elegant morning garden-party buffet or an informal kitchen table setting enjoyed with a special friend, these dishes will forever change the way you look at breakfast. You may never want to skip the morning meal again.

Life in a Country Inn

Perhaps some people's lives follow a carefully laid-out course, where thoughtful decisions are made based on fact and research, but my path is at best an educated yet haphazard zigzag of sentiment and naïveté. I believe therein lies the making of an innkeeper. It is ridiculous to give up the security of earning a fine wage with paid vacations and retirement annuities, to live without daily newspaper delivery, midnight delis and even harsher deprivations, to welcome complete strangers into your home. This is the path I chose as a country innkeeper/chef in the late 1980s. The marvelous part of this particular story is that it led to success.

My husband Bob and I began this journey at the start of our marriage. Thinking about purchasing a vacation home on the Maine coast, and not knowing exactly how to pay for it, we came up with the brilliant idea of creating an inn. After all, we were staying in one at the time, which just about made us experts. At this point in my life, I was a successful self-employed video producer, and my husband was (and continues to be) a professor at a major urban university. Using the equity in our year-round home as collateral, we purchased a summer home in Maine—what we now call our "practice" inn, since we only lived and worked there each year for the brief summer season. (Maine joke: There are only two seasons in Maine—winter and the Fourth of July.)

Our move to the country and to what has become the Inn at Twin Linden took place during one of our winters as off-season Maine innkeepers. Since we maintained our permanent residence and employment in the Philadelphia area, we decided to look for a property that might one day be our "real" inn. In our usual shotgun style, the first and only property we looked at and the one we purchased that winter was a rundown estate in Lancaster County (Pennsylvania's Dutch Country). Three years and numerous sagas later, the estate had been converted to what is now the Inn at Twin Linden. Our inn is in a small rural town surrounded by Amish and Mennonite farmers, a country inn in the truest sense.

Country life is a many-faceted existence that requires enormous flexibility and patience, but it is most of all an inherently joyous life-style that celebrates moments of each day. For an innkeeper, country life means taking on more responsibilities along with obvious rewards. There is no litmus test for becoming an innkeeper, but my general rule is: If you excel at one specific task, you probably should remain in your field, for your own benefit and for that of society. If, on the other hand, you excel at many things and don't mind somewhat schizophrenically switching from one task to the next to the next (or better, if, like my husband, you actually prefer this approach), then innkeeping could be your thing. We think of innkeeping as the inability to ever get anywhere in a straight line. There is always something to be done along the way, perhaps a moment to enjoy the sunrise, which is conveniently on the way to picking some herbs, which happens to be going by the bird-feeders that need to be filled. And so it goes.

Another paramount requirement of country-inn living is self-sufficiency. Often your schedule keeps you from locating sources of particular needed items; sometimes it is sheer geography that prevents you from them. Whatever the reason, you learn to do a lot of things yourself. The most conspicuous way that I go "solo" is in my duties as chef. In fact, I constitute the entire cooking staff. I have no sous chef, no pastry chef—no one to come in early and prep, no one to go to market in search of fresh produce or meat. Much like your own home kitchen, my kitchen is my domain—anything that comes from it is my responsibility alone.

However, for several reasons, we do not grow our own fruits and vegetables at the inn. First, I don't have the time to do a good job of it. Anyone who's had a home garden knows it becomes an all-encompassing task just getting the soil ready and planted. Add on to that the tasks of upkeep and a few unfriendly bugs or fungi, and you're into a full-time occupation. Second, the local Amish and Mennonite farmers have had a lot more practice at this. As a matter of fact, they're truly experts. They know which strains grow best in our soil, what pests are good and how to eliminate the bad ones, when to plant and pick, etc. Occasionally I lose my head and buy a few plants for things that I don't see at the farmstands, but I've learned that a better approach is to ask a local farmer to grow those products for me. So in the spring, I'm an anxious spectator, dabbling in the world of the flower and herb gardens, but appreciatively awaiting the work of the pros for fresh produce to put on my table and menus.

Our inn kitchen is smaller than many "gourmet" home kitchens I've seen, with limited storage and cooking space. We have no walk-in refrigerators and no multiple ovens—I use a six-burner commercial gas stove, a salamander broiler/grill, and a single gas convection oven. We have no steam table, although we do have a heat lamp, which is used only during breakfast to keep our fresh-baked items warm. I still miss my old-fashioned wood-burning cookstove with its warming shelf in our Maine inn. Since we have only one oven, my menus must be planned so that all baked items can be cooked at the same temperature—just like at home. And more burners on the stove might lead to more pots going at once than a single chef can reasonably tend. As a result of this experience, my breakfast recipes are perfectly adaptable for the home kitchen.

When we were contemplating what our reputation at the Inn at Twin Linden might rest on, we looked back over our guest comments and letters from Maine. Overwhelmingly, our food and, in particular, our breakfasts were the most memorable aspects of the experience that our guests took home with them. The recipes and menus that follow all helped to establish our reputation for incredible breakfasts.

About Our Area

The farmland in the valleys around our inn is the most fertile nonirrigated land in the country. At the time when William Penn offered freedom from religious persecution in a New World, the forefathers of our Amish and Mennonite farmers (often referred to as "Plain People") chose this land because of that fact. Farming here is more than an occupation, it is a legacy, a framework for attaining a higher end, the past and the future all tied together in everyday life. To understand our country life and the references I make to our Plain neighbors, it is perhaps important to know something about the Plain culture that surrounds us and to differentiate among its groups.

In Lancaster County, we have many different sects of the religious groups commonly called "Mennonite" or "Amish." While the religious beliefs of these groups are a study in themselves, our relationship to them is perhaps more culturally based. In this sense, although the religious differences give us the "why" of their behavior, the social structure of the Plain People is the thing that most affects us. There are two main groups of Plain People in Lancaster County—the Amish and the Mennonites. (The word *Amish* comes from the leader Jacob Amman; *Mennonite,* from leader Menno Simons.) In simplistic terms, the strictest group of Plain People are known as Amish. The Amish believe that anything tying them to the modern world is negative, and that belief can be seen in their homes and in their farming methods. They have no modern plumbing or electricity and therefore no electric appliances, like refrigerators or freezers, and no electric lights. They do sometimes have gas generators to run equipment. Their farming is generally done by hand, either with horse-drawn implements like plows and/or manual labor. They have no cars and no telephones, although they sometimes ride in non-Amish or "English" persons' cars or use public telephones. The Amish wear dark, solid colors, and they do not have churches or meeting houses but prefer to hold religious services in the members' homes. In our area, the Amish buggies are gray, while in other communities, even in other parts of Pennsylvania, different colors are used.

The Mennonites include many different groups of varying degrees of "worldliness." The Old Order, what we refer to as "Buggy" Mennonites, are the strictest (their buggies are black). Others are "black car" Mennonites (they may have cars, but they must be black—as far as I know, a black Mercedes is quite acceptable); "black bumper" Mennonites (black cars with bumpers and chrome painted black); and "regular car" Mennonites (any model or color). Some of the Mennonites use tractors; some use horse-drawn plows; and some use combinations. Some also will not use the tractors themselves, but it's acceptable for them to hire workers to use them on their land.

Mennonites meet in churches or meeting houses. Some have electricity, but may restrict its use—it might be allowed in a barn or workshop, for example, but not in the home. Their dress varies as well: most wear head coverings, and many sects require that women wear dresses at all times.

Confused? While the lines between the various groups are somewhat murky to the layperson, there are common threads that run through and tie together all levels of the Plain culture. The Plain People take the idea of "family values" to its highest level. Children are cherished in ways different from what is customary in our culture. Parents take the obligation to prepare children for adulthood very seriously, and so the children learn the work ethic at an amazingly early age. It is not uncommon to see five-year-old boys plowing the fields with their fathers and ten-year-olds driving tractors. Little girls hang laundry, sweep the porch with brooms twice their size, and as young women learn to quilt and sew.

Foremost, the Amish and Mennonite people are tied together by their bond with the land. Farming as a way of life maintains order in these communities—the change of seasons and the dependency upon each other to bring crops to harvest promotes the Plain ideals of hard work and self-sufficiency in the community and family as a means to a higher spiritual end. As part of the area in which they live, we are privileged to benefit from their dedication to the rural life on a daily basis, from the quality dairy and poultry products we use year-round to our extraordinary access to fresh-from-the-vines-and-fields crops in season. At the finest restaurants in nearby Philadelphia and other large metropolitan areas, the sure sign of quality ingredients on a menu is the label "fresh from Lancaster County." Thanks to the dedication of our Plain People, our choice of Lancaster County as the location for our country inn has enabled us to provide the exceptional quality of ingredients that enhances our emphasis on cuisine.

Beyond Muffins—Baked Goods for Breakfast

Starting off the morning meal with a special baked item lets the guest know right away that this will be no ordinary breakfast. Although I have nothing against muffins, I regard them more as an accompaniment to a meal (like the bread or rolls served with dinner) rather than the equivalent of a first course. Many muffins are also often laden with "hidden" calories and fat, especially when accompanied by butter and jam. These recipes are for a taste of something wonderful that will awaken the palate to the special meal that lies ahead.

Cranberry Apple Pecan Bread Pudding with Vanilla Bean Custard

Lemon Soufflé with Blueberry Swirl

Raisin Scones with Lemon Curd

Croissant Cinnamon Raisin Buns

Wild Blueberry Bread

Raspberry Lemon Turnovers

Hazelnut Cinnamon Biscotti

Strawberry Cream Puffs with Mascarpone and Fresh Berry Coulis

Coffee Chocolate Pecan Popovers

Cranberry Pear Clafouti

Apple Cheese Tart with Raisins and Walnuts

Blueberry Almond Tart with Frangipane

Almond Pear Tart with Apricot Glaze

Apple Cranberry Lattice Tart

Peach Fritters with Almond Cream

Blueberry Peach Cobbler with Cinnamon Sugar

Apple Walnut Streusel Cake with Cinnamon Custard

Blackberry Cream Streusel Cake with Cinnamon Cream

Peach Streusel Coffeecake

Carrot, Pumpkin and Pecan Cakes with Orange Filling

Lemon Poppy Seed Sandwiches with Lemon Cream Filling

Baked Apple with Oatmeal, Cinnamon and Pecans in Phyllo

Creamy Arborio Rice Pudding with Amaretto and Caramelized Sugar

Cranberry Apple Pecan Bread Pudding with Vanilla Bean Custard

Bread Pudding

- *1½ cups peeled and sliced baking apples*
- *2 teaspoons lemon juice*
- *4 large eggs*
- *¼ cup sugar*
- *2 teaspoons vanilla extract*
- *1 teaspoon freshly grated nutmeg*
- *1 teaspoon cinnamon*
- *¼ cup unsalted butter, melted*
- *2 cups half-and-half*
- *¼ cup brandy*
- *½ cup cranberries*
- *½ cup pecans*
- *5 cups stale croissants and brioche, cut in cubes*

Vanilla Bean Custard

- *2 cups half-and-half*
- *1 vanilla bean, split lengthwise*
- *6 egg yolks*
- *½ cup sugar*
- *2 teaspoons vanilla extract*

SERVES 6

Often our return guests bring us gifts, and one of my favorites was a huge basket of fresh Cape Cod cranberries, which were immediately put to use in this bread pudding.

Pudding: In a medium bowl, toss sliced apples with lemon juice and set aside. In the large bowl of an electric mixer, beat the eggs until frothy and light in color. Add the sugar, vanilla, nutmeg and cinnamon and beat until smooth. Stir in the butter, half-and-half and brandy. Toss the apples, cranberries and pecans with the bread cubes. Place the bread mixture in a greased 9 × 5-inch loaf pan (or individual custard cups). Pour the egg mixture evenly over the bread. Cover with foil and weigh down the top with a 1- or 2-lb. bag of rice or dried beans to encourage the bread to absorb the liquid. Refrigerate for 1 hour.

Preheat oven to 325° F. Remove the foil and weights and place the pudding in a larger pan with 1 inch of hot water. Bake for 55 minutes or until set. Increase oven temperature to 425° F and bake 10 minutes more, until lightly browned. Serve warm with room-temperature custard sauce.

Custard: Place the half-and-half and vanilla bean in a medium saucepan. Heat over medium heat until half-and-half is just about to boil. Remove from heat. In a metal mixing bowl, whisk together the egg yolks and sugar until light-colored. Remove the vanilla bean from the half-and-half and scrape the tiny seeds inside the pod into the half-and-half. Pour the half-and-half into the mixture and whisk in the vanilla.

Prepare a large bowl with ice and water and have a second smaller bowl ready. Return the mixture to the saucepan and cook over low heat, stirring constantly, until it just begins to thicken and coat the spoon. Immediately remove the mixture from the heat and pour into the empty bowl. Submerge the bottom of the bowl into the ice water to stop the custard from cooking and to prevent curdling; stir until cooled slightly. Cool for about 10 minutes longer.

Notes: Though bread pudding was created as a way to use barely edible scraps, using better bread enhances the quality of the pudding.

The custard may be made up to two days in advance and stored, covered, in the refrigerator. The bread pudding may be made up to 48 hours in advance, refrigerated, and reheated in a hot-water bath.

Lemon Soufflé with Blueberry Swirl

½ cup sugar
4 tablespoons butter
¾ cup fresh lemon juice
4 large egg yolks
½ cup half-and-half
1 cup fresh blueberries
6 large egg whites

SERVES 6

An elegant soufflé enhanced by fresh blueberries, this lemony treat must be served immediately for your guests to enjoy its full, "puffy" effect.

Preheat oven to 425° F. Butter 6 individual soufflé pans, sprinkle them with sugar, and tap out excess sugar; refrigerate until ready to use. In a medium saucepan, combine ¼ cup sugar, the butter and ½ cup lemon juice over medium heat. Cook until the mixture is well combined and the butter is melted. Remove from the heat and whisk in the egg yolks. Return the mixture to the heat and cook on low heat until slightly thickened, about 3 minutes; remove from the heat and keep warm.

Scald the half-and-half and whisk it into the lemon mixture. Return the lemon mixture to the heat and cook, stirring constantly, for 2 minutes, until thickened but not boiling. In a blender or food processor, process the remaining ¼ cup lemon juice and the blueberries until smooth. Beat the eggs whites until frothy. Continue to beat the whites while slowly sifting in the remaining sugar until they form soft, glossy peaks. Fold one-quarter of the egg whites into the blueberry mixture. Gently stir about one-quarter of the egg whites into the lemon mixture, then fold in the remaining egg whites until just combined. Swirl the blueberry mixture into the lemon mixture, folding just once. Spoon the soufflé into the prepared dishes, smoothing the surface of each. Bake on the lower rack of the oven for 10 to 12 minutes, until puffed and lightly browned. Sprinkle with confectioner's sugar and serve immediately.

NOTES: Soufflés require a consistent baking temperature and therefore should not be disturbed while baking. Resist the temptation to peek at them early on, since opening the oven door may cause enough of a temperature drop for them to fall. Overbaking the soufflés may also have the same effect.

To give the soufflés additional height, make collars for the soufflé pans by cutting 6 pieces of waxed paper or aluminum foil about 8 inches long each and folding them in thirds. Butter one side of each collar and wrap it, buttered side in, around the top of the cup. Tie a piece of string around the collar to hold it snugly on the cup (or if using foil, crimp the ends firmly together).

Raisin Scones with Lemon Curd

Scones

2 cups all-purpose flour

2½ teaspoons baking powder

½ teaspoon salt

½ teaspoon baking soda

6 tablespoons butter

½ cup raisins

1 egg

½ cup buttermilk

¼ cup milk

2 tablespoons sugar

Lemon Curd

Makes about 1½ cups

6 egg yolks

½ cup fresh lemon juice

½ cup butter

¾ cup sugar

MAKES ABOUT 1½ DOZEN SCONES

Delicate scones, the perfect accompaniment to tea, also make a tasty breakfast treat. This creamy lemon curd is easy to make.

Scones: Preheat oven to 425° F. Lightly grease a large baking sheet. Combine the flour, baking powder, salt and baking soda in a large bowl. Cut in the butter with a pastry blender until the mixture is crumbly. Mix in the raisins. Beat together the egg and buttermilk. Make a well in the center of the flour mixture and pour in the egg mixture. Mix with a wooden spoon until just combined.

Turn the dough onto a lightly floured board and knead gently for 1 minute. Roll out the dough ½ inch thick with a floured rolling pin. Cut the dough into 2-inch rounds (or use a small cookie cutter of your choice) and place on the greased sheet. Lightly brush the tops with the milk and sprinkle on the sugar. Bake 10 to 12 minutes or until lightly browned. Serve warm.

Lemon Curd: Combine all the ingredients in a small saucepan and place over medium heat, stirring constantly until the butter is melted. Lower the heat and continue to cook until the mixture thickens and is close to but not boiling (the egg yolks will curdle if they become too hot). Remove from heat and cool to room temperature. Refrigerate, covered, until ready to use.

Notes: The lemon curd will keep for up to 1 week. The scones may be made up to 1 day ahead but are best still warm from the oven.

The clotted cream that is traditionally served with scones can be made by bringing heavy cream just to a boil and then reducing it by approximately one half over low heat; cool the cream thoroughly before serving. Or, make your own quick home version of cream topping by whipping heavy cream to soft peaks and incorporating a little sugar and some bits of soft butter.

Croissant Cinnamon Raisin Buns

Dough

- *4 cups all-purpose flour*
- *2 packages active dry yeast*
- *⅓ cup warm water*
- *¼ cup plus 1 tablespoon sugar*
- *1 teaspoon salt*
- *2½ cups milk*
- *½ cup chilled butter, cut into bits*

Syrup and Filling

- *1 cup brown sugar*
- *¼ cup corn syrup*
- *½ cup granulated sugar*
- *2 tablespoons cinnamon*
- *4 tablespoons butter, cut into bits*
- *½ cup raisins*

Topping

- *½ cup granulated sugar*
- *½ cup brown sugar*
- *¼ cup all-purpose flour*
- *2 tablespoons cinnamon*
- *4 tablespoons butter, cut in small pieces*

Assembly

- *1 egg*
- *1 tablespoon water*

MAKES 12 BUNS

The aroma of these buns sometimes draws people to my kitchen door in hopes of buying some.

Dough: Place 1 cup flour in a bowl. Dissolve yeast and 1 tablespoon sugar in the warm water and allow to proof for 5 minutes (active yeast will cause bubbles to form on the surface). Stir the yeast mixture into the flour to form a soft dough, adding more warm water if necessary. Leave in a warm place for 30 minutes or until doubled in volume.

Mix the remaining 3 cups flour with ¼ cup sugar, salt and milk to make a dough. Add the yeast-risen mixture and mix well. Roll out the dough thinly—no more than about ⅛ inch thick—and dot it with the butter. Fold the dough into three, as you would a letter. (This is the first "turn.") Roll out again, then fold into three again. Chill for 30 minutes. Make two further "turns," refrigerating dough in between as necessary to prevent the butter from melting. Refrigerate the dough until you are ready to assemble the buns.

Syrup and Filling: In a medium saucepan, combine ½ cup brown sugar and corn syrup over low heat just until the sugar is melted; set aside to cool slightly. Combine the granulated and remaining ½ cup brown sugar. Mix in the cinnamon. With a pastry blender or two knives, cut in butter until crumbled. Mix in the raisins.

Topping: Combine granulated sugar, brown sugar, flour and cinnamon. With a pastry blender or two knives, cut in the butter until crumbled. Refrigerate until ready to use.

Assembly: Roll the dough out to a rectangle approximately 8 × 24 inches and about ¼ inch thick. Spread the syrup evenly over the rectangle and then sprinkle evenly with the filling mixture. Cut the dough into 12 2 × 8-inch strips. Roll each strip up and place 6 rolls into each of two lightly greased 9 × 13 × 2-inch pans.

Cover the pans with towels and allow buns to rise in a slightly humid warm place (I use a pan of steaming water in my gas oven with just the heat from the pilot), until tripled in volume (1 to 1½ hours).

Preheat oven to 375° F. Whisk together the egg and water and lightly brush the tops of the buns with the mixture. Bake for 15 minutes. Remove from oven, sprinkle with the topping mixture and bake for approximately 15 minutes more. When done, the topping will be crumbled but firm, and the buns will be browned on sides. Serve warm.

Notes: Frozen croissant dough, available from specialty shops, can be substituted. Defrost it according to package directions.

Buns may be covered and refrigerated overnight. Allow 15 minutes to come to room temperature before placing in oven.

Dough may be made up to 2 days ahead.

The buns may also be frozen, unbaked and well wrapped, for up to a month before the final rising. I typically defrost the buns in the refrigerator overnight and do the last rising in the morning.

Wild Blueberry Bread

Bread

- *¼ cup butter, softened*
- *½ cup sugar*
- *2 large eggs*
- *2 cups unsifted all-purpose flour*
- *2 teaspoons baking powder*
- *¼ teaspoon salt*
- *⅓ cup milk*
- *1 teaspoon vanilla extract*
- *2 teaspoons grated lemon peel*
- *1 cup wild Maine blueberries*

Cinnamon Mixture

- *⅓ cup sugar*
- *¼ cup brown sugar*
- *¼ cup all-purpose flour*
- *2 teaspoons cinnamon*
- *2 tablespoons cold butter, cut into bits*

SERVES 6 TO 8

This bread is also delicious made with dried wild blueberries, which have a chewy raisinlike texture.

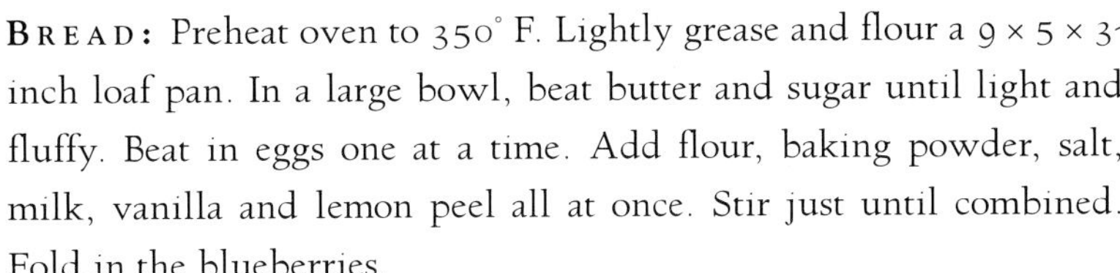

Bread: Preheat oven to 350° F. Lightly grease and flour a 9 × 5 × 3-inch loaf pan. In a large bowl, beat butter and sugar until light and fluffy. Beat in eggs one at a time. Add flour, baking powder, salt, milk, vanilla and lemon peel all at once. Stir just until combined. Fold in the blueberries.

Cinnamon Mixture: In a small mixing bowl, combine sugar, brown sugar, flour and cinnamon. Cut in butter with a pastry blender until crumbly.

Assembly: Turn ½ of the batter into the prepared pan. Sprinkle ½ of the cinnamon mixture over top. With a butter knife, swirl cinnamon mixture into batter about 1 inch deep. Spoon remaining batter on top. Sprinkle with remaining cinnamon mixture and swirl lightly again. Bake until golden on top and a toothpick comes out clean, 55 to 60 minutes. Cool in pan 5 minutes; turn onto cooling rack and cool.

Notes: This is a great "do-ahead" recipe that can be executed the night before and reheated in a microwave oven if desired. Of course, it's wonderful fresh from the oven and equally perfect for afternoon tea.

The bread also freezes well, up to 1 month. If fresh Maine blueberries are unavailable, substitute cultivated blueberries. Frozen blueberries may also be used. Slices of the bread are delicious toasted or grilled with butter.

Raspberry Lemon Turnovers

Pastry Dough

1½ cups all-purpose flour
¼ teaspoon salt
½ teaspoon cinnamon
2 tablespoons sugar
2 tablespoons solid vegetable shortening
3 tablespoons chilled unsalted butter, cut into bits
2 to 3 tablespoons cold water

Filling

1½ cups raspberries
½ cup sugar
2 teaspoons lemon juice
2 tablespoons cornstarch
2 tablespoons lemon zest

Assembly

1 egg
1 teaspoon water

SERVES 6

OPPOSITE: *Raisin Scones with Lemon Curd; Raspberry Lemon Turnovers; Hazelnut Cinnamon Biscotti*

IN ALL MANIFESTATIONS, LEMON AND RASPBERRIES MAKE a happy pairing. These turnovers are smaller than the more familiar bake-shop specimens, which makes them good in combination with other baked treats.

DOUGH: In a medium bowl, combine the flour, salt, cinnamon and sugar. Using a pastry blender, cut in the shortening and butter until crumbly. Sprinkle on the water 1 teaspoon at a time while tossing mixture to combine, adding just enough water to be able to mold the dough into a well-formed ball. Divide evenly into 6 balls and refrigerate until ready to use.

FILLING: In a medium saucepan, combine 1 cup raspberries, sugar, lemon juice and cornstarch. Heat over low heat for 2 minutes, stirring constantly to avoid sticking. Increase heat to medium and cook until a syrup begins to bubble and thicken, 3 to 5 minutes. Remove the mixture from the heat and gently stir in the remaining ½ cup raspberries and the lemon zest. Cool to room temperature.

ASSEMBLY: Preheat oven to 425° F. Whisk together egg and water and set aside. Roll each ball of dough out between sheets of waxed paper into a 3½-inch round or square. Place equal amounts of the raspberry filling in the center of each piece of dough. Fold the pastry over and press the edges together to seal. Prick the tops with a fork and set on an ungreased baking sheet. Brush each turnover with egg wash and bake for 15 to 20 minutes, until light brown. Cool slightly before serving, as the filling will be hot.

NOTES: Frozen puff pastry is a quick and easy alternative to the pastry crust.

The finished turnovers or just the pastry dough may be made up to 24 hours ahead and kept in the refrigerator tightly wrapped with plastic wrap.

Try different berries, like blackberries or blueberries, for the filling.

Divide the dough into 12 smaller balls for miniature turnovers, perfect for a buffet table when guests typically want a little taste of everything.

Histoire Naturelle

Hazelnut Cinnamon Biscotti

1 cup hazelnuts
2 ¾ cups all-purpose flour
2 cups sugar
½ cup finely ground hazelnuts
½ teaspoon salt
1 teaspoon baking powder
3 tablespoons unsalted butter, cut into bits
3 eggs
3 egg yolks
1 teaspoon vanilla extract
2 teaspoons cinnamon
2 tablespoons melted butter

MAKES 36 TO 40 BISCOTTI

The perfect accompaniment to a freshly brewed cup of coffee or espresso, the biscotti begins the morning meal with a not-overly-sweet crunch and is a terrific "do-ahead" item—perfect for a picnic-basket breakfast. This recipe is a fairly traditional one, in that the biscotti are "twice baked," first in small loaves, then cut into slices and returned to the oven to be toasted. What makes these biscotti unique is that they also are "twice dipped"—in cinnamon sugar—for a delicious crunchy treat.

Preheat oven to 350° F. Toast the hazelnuts on a baking sheet for 10 minutes. Cool slightly, then rub in towels to remove skins.

In a large mixing bowl, combine the flour, 1½ cups of sugar, the ground hazelnuts, salt and baking powder. Cut in the butter with a pastry blender (or use a food processor) until crumbly. Whisk together the eggs, egg yolks and vanilla. Mix the egg mixture into the dry ingredients until just combined. Chop the toasted nuts very coarsely and stir them into the mixture.

Turn the mixture onto a lightly floured work surface and knead for 2 to 3 minutes. Add flour as necessary to make the dough easy to handle. Divide the dough into 3 balls. Roll each ball out to a log about 10 inches long and 1½ inches wide.

In a shallow bowl, combine the remaining ½ cup sugar and the cinnamon. Roll the tops of each log in the cinnamon-sugar mixture and place them on a baking sheet lined with lightly greased parchment. Bake for 30 to 35 minutes, until lightly browned but still slightly soft to the touch. Remove the logs from the oven and reduce the oven temperature to 300° F. Cool the logs for 5 minutes.

Cut the logs into ½- to ¾-inch-thick slices and lay the slices flat on the baking sheet. Return the slices to the oven and bake another 10 to 12 minutes, until they just begin to brown. Cool the biscotti on a baking rack for 10 minutes.

Brush the top side of each piece with a little melted butter and dip in the remaining cinnamon-sugar mixture. Allow to dry for 5 minutes, then store in an airtight container lined with waxed paper.

Note: Biscotti will keep for several weeks in an airtight container.

Strawberry Cream Puffs with Mascarpone and Fresh Berry Coulis

Cream Puffs

- *½ cup water*
- *¼ cup butter*
- *½ cup all-purpose flour*
- *2 eggs*

Filling

- *½ cup mascarpone cheese*
- *¼ cup ricotta cheese*
- *¼ cup sugar*
- *2 teaspoons lemon juice*
- *2 cups strawberries, sliced and hulled*

Coulis

- *2 cups strawberries, hulled*
- *¼ cup raspberries*
- *2 tablespoons sugar (optional)*
- *2 tablespoons orange juice*

SERVES 6

If a cream puff means dessert to you, think again of its components—butter, flour, egg—a classic breakfast combination. The creamy filling in this case is made with mascarpone and ricotta, and the natural sweetness in the coulis comes from seasonal ripe berries.

Cream Puffs: Preheat oven to 400° F. In a medium saucepan, heat water and butter to a boil. Add the flour, beating vigorously until the mixture forms a ball. Remove from heat. With an electric mixer, beat in the eggs until smooth. Drop 3 tablespoons of dough onto an ungreased baking sheet to form each shell, spacing puffs 3 inches apart. Bake for 35 minutes or until golden brown. Remove the sheet from the oven, cut off the top third of the puffs, lay the tops next to the bottoms and return the sheet to the oven for 5 minutes to dry out the centers.

Filling: Whisk together the mascarpone, ricotta, sugar and lemon juice. Divide the mixture among the cream puffs. Divide the strawberries among the puffs and spoon them over the cream filling.

Coulis: Process all the ingredients together in a food processor or blender until smooth. Pour the coulis onto 6 individual plates and set a puff on each.

Notes: Don't let generalizations about seasonality intimidate you in selecting produce; the best test of how delicious a fruit or vegetable is is to taste it yourself. Local seasonal fruit is usually the freshest and best tasting, but today's farmers deserve credit for growing wonderfully tasty fruit and vegetables in all areas of our country—and sometimes even outside of the country. Produce can be shipped within hours of harvesting, which makes it accessible to everyone.

The unfilled cream puffs may be made up to 24 hours in advance and stored in an airtight container. If excessive humidity causes them to soften, reheat them in a 400° F oven for 3 to 5 minutes. Cool before filling. Try different berries for the filling and coulis.

Coffee Chocolate Pecan Popovers

2 eggs
1 cup milk
2 tablespoons instant coffee
1 cup all-purpose flour
½ teaspoon salt
½ cup semi-sweet chocolate, chopped into fine bits
1 cup finely ground pecans

SERVES 6

THE DECADENT FEELING OF EATING CHOCOLATE FOR breakfast is balanced by the light-as-air quality of these popovers.

Preheat oven to 450° F. Grease 6 popover pans or large muffin cups. In a medium bowl, beat eggs lightly. In a separate bowl, whisk together the milk and instant coffee and pour into the eggs. Add the flour and salt and beat until just smooth. Gently fold in chocolate bits and pecans. Divide the batter among the cups. Bake for 20 minutes. Decrease oven temperature to 350° F and bake 15 minutes longer. Remove from oven and immediately remove from pans. Serve hot.

NOTES: Popovers should be served warm from the oven while they're still puffed. Finely chopping the chocolate and walnuts prevents the weight of these ingredients from collapsing the popover.

Try different nuts (walnuts, hazelnuts, etc.) for a unique variation. While popover pans may seem like an extravagant purchase, the shape of the pans creates a dramatic pouf on top that makes a fabulous and elegant presentation. Perhaps that's why Nieman Marcus serves its version with lunch.

Cranberry Pear Clafouti

2 eggs
⅓ cup sugar
3 tablespoons all-purpose flour
⅔ cup half-and-half
3 tablespoons butter, melted
4 pears, peeled, halved and cored
½ cup cranberries

SERVES 6 TO 8

CLAFOUTI IS A BAKED FRUIT CUSTARD; THIS FALL/WINTER version features cranberries and pears but any firm ripe fruit will work well. Try black cherries for the traditional summer version or sweet strawberries in the spring.

Preheat oven to 375° F; butter a 9-inch glass pie pan. In a medium bowl, whisk together the eggs and sugar until lightly colored. Whisk in the flour and half-and-half. Stir in the butter. Pour the mixture into the prepared pan. Carefully arrange the pear halves, cut side down, in a circle in the batter and spoon the cranberries between each. Bake for 25 to 30 minutes or until the pears are tender and the custard is lightly browned. Let cool slightly and serve.

Apple Cheese Tart with Raisins and Walnuts

Crust

- 1 cup butter
- ½ cup sugar
- 2 egg yolks
- 1 teaspoon lemon juice
- 2¼ cups all-purpose flour
- 1½ teaspoons baking powder
- Pinch of salt

Cheese Mixture

- 12 oz. cream cheese, at room temperature
- 1 teaspoon vanilla extract
- ¼ cup sugar
- 2 eggs

Toppings

- 3 large cooking apples, peeled, cored and sliced into ¼ inch wedges
- 2 tablespoons lemon juice
- ⅓ cup sugar
- 1 teaspoon cinnamon
- ½ cup golden raisins
- ½ cup chopped walnuts
- ½ cup brown sugar
- 2 tablespoons all-purpose flour

Assembly

- 2 tablespoons butter, cut into bits

SERVES 6 TO 8

We get many varieties of our own locally grown apples from Weaver's Orchards, where they also press fresh apple cider while you wait. Apples are one of our last local harvests in fall, a time of celebration for the farmers and the community. This apple-cheese tart combines sophisticated taste with old-fashioned pleasure.

Crust: Preheat oven to 350° F. With an electric mixer, cream together the butter and sugar. Add the egg yolks and lemon juice and beat until smooth. Add the flour, baking powder and salt and mix until just combined. On a floured surface, roll out the dough into a 12- to 13-inch circle. Transfer and fit into a 9- or 10-inch tart pan with a removable bottom. Refrigerate until needed.

Cheese Mixture: Beat the cheese with an electric mixer until smooth. Add the vanilla and sugar and beat until combined. Beat in the eggs one at a time, scraping down the sides of the bowl; set aside.

Toppings: Toss the apples with the lemon juice to prevent them from browning, then toss with the sugar and cinnamon. In a separate bowl, combine the golden raisins, walnuts, brown sugar and flour.

Assembly: Preheat oven to 350° F. Spread the cheese mixture evenly into the crust. Arrange the apple slices in a circular pattern on top, beginning at the center and working out. Sprinkle the raisin mixture over the apples and dot with the butter. Cover loosely with foil and bake for 20 minutes. Remove the foil and bake for 20 minutes more, until golden brown. Serve warm.

Notes: I prefer slightly tart baking apples, like Rome or McIntosh, for this recipe.

The crust has a delicious shortbread taste and consistency.

The tart may be prepared 48 hours in advance and rewarmed for serving.

Blueberry Almond Tart with Frangipane

Frangipane

- *¾ cup milk*
- *1 vanilla bean (or 2 teaspoons vanilla extract)*
- *½ cup all-purpose flour*
- *½ cup sugar*
- *2 beaten egg yolks*
- *⅓ cup crushed macaroons*
- *2 tablespoons butter, softened*

Crust

- *½ lb. unsalted butter*
- *½ cup sugar*
- *2 egg yolks*
- *1 teaspoon almond extract*
- *1 teaspoon grated lemon zest*
- *2¼ cups all-purpose flour*
- *1½ teaspoons baking powder*

Blueberry Filling

- *½ cup sugar*
- *⅓ cup all-purpose flour*
- *1½ tablespoons cornstarch*
- *3 cups blueberries*
- *1 teaspoon lemon juice*

Assembly

- *2 tablespoons butter*
- *¼ cup confectioner's sugar for dusting*

SERVES 6 TO 8

THIS RECIPE BRINGS BACK MEMORIES OF OUR FIRST INN IN Maine, where one of the few fresh fruits available all summer was the local crop of wild blueberries. Although there are commercial blueberry barrens—Maine for "farms"—these tiny gems cannot be cultivated but grow wild along the roadsides. We would return from picking with blue fingertips and blue lips and would indulge ourselves in everything blueberry through the short season.

If wild blueberries aren't available, never mind—the almond cream in this recipe will enhance the flavor of big cultivated ones.

FRANGIPANE: In a medium saucepan, bring the milk with the vanilla bean in it to a boil. Remove the bean and set the milk aside. In another saucepan, combine the flour, sugar, and beaten egg yolks. Gradually add the hot milk until combined. Cook slowly over low heat, stirring constantly, until the cream thickens. Pour the cream into a bowl and stir in the crushed macaroons and the softened butter. Set aside to cool to room temperature.

CRUST: Preheat oven to 350° F. Using a mixer, cream together the butter and sugar. Add the egg yolks, almond extract, and lemon zest. Beat until smooth. Add the flour and baking powder and mix well.

Using a 9- or 10-inch tart pan with a removable bottom, press ⅔ of the dough in the bottom of the pan with your fingers, and work the dough up the rim about ½ inch. Set the remaining dough aside.

FILLING: In a medium bowl, mix together the sugar, flour and cornstarch. Stir in the blueberries, sprinkle with lemon and toss to coat the blueberries evenly.

ASSEMBLY: Spread an even layer of frangipane in the bottom of the crust, using just enough to cover. Pour in the blueberry mixture and dot the top with 2 tablespoons of butter. On a floured surface, roll out the remaining dough to 3/16 inch thick. Cut strips of dough ½ inch wide and arrange them diagonally, ½ inch apart, to form a lattice top. Trim away any overhanging dough.

Bake the tart for 40 minutes or until lightly browned. Dust with powdered sugar and serve warm.

NOTES: The frangipane may be prepared up to 24 hours ahead and stored in the refrigerator. Ready-made frangipane, available from specialty food shops, can be substituted.

Ground almonds may be substituted for the crushed macaroons.

The tart may be baked up to 24 hours ahead, stored in the refrigerator, and reheated in a 350° F oven for 8 minutes before serving.

While fresh blueberries are preferred, frozen blueberries are an acceptable substitute if fresh are unavailable.

Almond Pear Tart with Apricot Glaze

CRUST

2 cups graham cracker crumbs
4 tablespoons sugar
¼ cup all-purpose flour
½ cup butter, melted

FILLING

1½ cups heavy cream
½ cup milk
¼ cup sugar
1 egg
4 egg yolks
1½ teaspoons almond extract
4 large pears, peeled, halved and cored

GLAZE

1½ cups apricot preserves

SERVES 6 TO 8

THE FABULOUS APPEARANCE OF THIS TART BELIES ITS simple preparation. I prefer Bosc or Comice pears for baking (and for eating), although any firm, sweet variety will work in this versatile tart.

CRUST: Preheat oven to 350° F. Mix crumbs, sugar, and flour together in a medium bowl. Stir in melted butter. Press the mixture firmly into the bottom and sides of a 9- or 10-inch tart pan with a removable bottom. Bake for 10 minutes. Set aside to cool completely.

FILLING: In a medium saucepan, scald the cream and remove from heat. Whisk together the sugar, egg and egg yolks in a metal mixing bowl until light colored. Slowly pour the hot cream mixture over the egg mixture and whisk to combine well. Stir in the almond extract.

ASSEMBLY: Pour the custard into the baked shell. Arrange the pear halves on the custard in a circular pattern; slash the pears crosswise if desired. Bake for about 25 minutes or until the custard is just set and the pears are tender. Allow the tart to cool.

Heat the apricot preserves in a small saucepan or microwave oven until liquefied. Strain the preserves through a fine sieve. Spoon the glaze over the cool tart and refrigerate until set. Reheat for 5 minutes or serve cold.

NOTES: Drop the pear halves into cold water with lemon juice to prevent browning.

The tart may be made up to 24 hours in advance and reheated (if desired) before serving. Do not heat the tart for longer than 5 minutes or the glaze will melt.

Apple Cranberry Lattice Tart

Crust

- ½ lb. butter
- ½ cup sugar
- 2 egg yolks
- 2¼ cups all-purpose flour
- ½ cup finely ground walnuts
- ½ teaspoon cinnamon
- ¼ teaspoon ground cloves
- 1 teaspoon baking powder

Filling

- 3 cups chopped apples
- 2 tablespoons lemon juice
- ½ cup cranberries
- ½ cup butter
- 1 cup sugar
- 2 tablespoons brown sugar
- ⅓ cup orange juice

Assembly

- 2 tablespoons butter
- 1 egg
- 2 tablespoons water

SERVES 6 TO 8

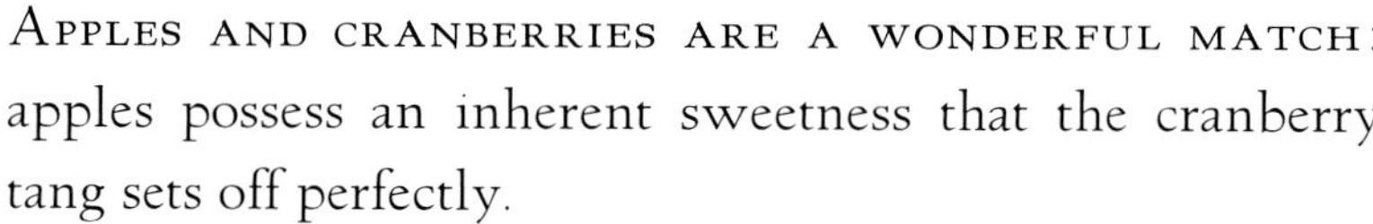

Apples and cranberries are a wonderful match: apples possess an inherent sweetness that the cranberry tang sets off perfectly.

Crust: Preheat oven to 350° F. Cream together the butter and sugar. Beat in the egg yolks until smooth. In a separate bowl, combine the flour, ground walnuts, cinnamon, cloves and baking powder. Add the dry mixture to the butter mixture and mix until just combined. Using a 4 × 14-inch rectangular mold (or a 9-inch tart pan with removable bottom), press ⅔ of the dough into the bottom and up the sides of the pan about ½ inch. Set aside.

Filling: In a medium bowl, toss the apples with the lemon juice to prevent them from browning. Add the cranberries and set aside. In a medium skillet, melt the butter over low heat. Add the sugar and brown sugar and cook for 1 to 2 minutes, until sugar starts to melt. Stir in the orange juice until combined. Add the apple-cranberry mixture and continue stirring with a wooden spoon until the fruit is coated and the mixture is bubbly, about 3 to 4 minutes. Remove from heat and allow to cool.

Assembly: Spread the apple mixture evenly in the crust; dot with the butter. Roll out the remaining dough approximately ¼ inch thick and cut into ¾-inch strips long enough to cover the tart. Arrange the strips diagonally ½ inch apart in a lattice pattern over the apple filling. Whisk together the egg and water and brush the strips lightly with the mixture. Bake for 40 minutes or until golden brown. Cool slightly before serving.

Notes: Tart may be baked up to 24 hours in advance and reheated for about 10 minutes before serving.

The filling also makes a tasty and easily prepared topping for pancakes or waffles.

Peach Fritters with Almond Cream

Almond Cream

- *½ cup mascarpone cheese*
- *¼ cup sugar*
- *1 teaspoon almond extract*
- *1 teaspoon amaretto*
- *1 cup heavy cream, whipped to soft peaks*

Fritters

- *6 peaches, peeled and pitted*
- *⅓ cup sugar*
- *⅓ cup brandy*
- *1 teaspoon cinnamon*
- *1 teaspoon baking powder*
- *1¾ cups all-purpose flour*
- *½ teaspoon salt*
- *2 eggs, separated*
- *1 cup milk*
- *2 tablespoons melted butter*
- *1 qt. corn oil for frying*

SERVES 10 TO 12

Fritters are fried—there's no getting around it—but they're a delicious treat when you're in the mood to indulge. In this version, the sweet peach filling and crunchy outer crust are delicious on their own, but add the mascarpone-based almond cream and you'll know you're not in Kansas anymore.

Almond Cream: With an electric mixer, blend the mascarpone and sugar until smooth. Add the almond extract and amaretto and combine well. Fold in ⅓ of the whipped cream to lighten the mixture, then fold in the remaining whipped cream. Keep almond cream refrigerated until ready to serve.

Fritters: Cut the peaches into 1-inch wedges. In a medium bowl, combine the sugar, brandy and cinnamon. Add the peaches and toss to coat. Set aside. In a large bowl, combine the baking powder, flour and salt. Whisk together the egg yolks and milk and stir the mixture into the dry ingredients. Stir in the butter.

Heat 1 inch of oil in a medium skillet or deep fryer to 375° F. Whip the egg whites to soft peaks and fold them into the batter. Dip each peach wedge into the batter, letting the excess drip back into the bowl. Drop into the hot oil and fry until browned (1 to 2 minutes per side). Drain the fritters on paper towels and keep them warm until all the peaches are used. Serve the fritters with dollops of almond cream.

Notes: Use sweet, ripe peaches for the best tasting fritter. Drop the dipped peaches into the hot oil with caution to avoid splashing. Fritters are best consumed immediately—but who could wait?

The almond cream may be made up to 24 hours in advance.

You may notice that mascarpone is used in various ways in different dishes throughout this book. Like crème fraîche, it gives a smooth creamy base to sweet and savory dishes alike; however, it does not have the tang of crème fraîche and can add a little more body to a dish because of its soft cream-cheese consistency.

FOLLOWING PAGES: *Peach Fritters with Almond Cream; Apple Walnut Streusel Cake with Cinnamon Custard; Apple Cranberry Lattice Tart; Blueberry Peach Cobbler with Cinnamon Sugar*

Blueberry Peach Cobbler with Cinnamon Sugar

Blueberry Peach Filling

- *¾ cup sugar*
- *¼ cup all-purpose flour*
- *½ teaspoon salt*
- *1 qt. fresh blueberries (about 1¾ cups)*
- *1 lb. fresh peaches, peeled, pitted and sliced (about 1½ cups)*
- *2 tablespoons lemon juice*
- *2 tablespoons butter*

Topping

- *1 cup all-purpose flour*
- *2 teaspoons baking powder*
- *¼ cup plus 2 tablespoons sugar*
- *½ teaspoon salt*
- *¼ cup cold butter, cut into bits*
- *⅓ cup milk*
- *1 egg, slightly beaten*
- *2 teaspoons cinnamon*

SERVES 6

Cobblers are among the home-style baked goods that have enjoyed a resurgence in popularity lately in fine restaurants around the country. This breakfast version depends on the ripeness of two of summer's sweetest fruits and is easy to prepare. A fresh fruit filling is baked in a hot oven till bubbly and the topping is dropped on to bake into a flaky biscuit. The flavor added by a sprinkling of cinnamon and sugar is reminiscent of the cinnamon toast enjoyed in childhood days.

Filling: Preheat oven to 400° F. Mix sugar, flour, and salt in a medium bowl. Add the blueberries, peaches, and lemon juice and toss the mixture to coat the fruit evenly. Divide the fruit mixture among 6 individual lightly greased ramekins. Place ramekins on a 9 x 13-inch baking sheet and bake for 15 minutes or until hot and bubbling.

Topping: While the fruit is baking, mix the topping. Sift together flour, baking powder, 2 tablespoons sugar, and salt. Cut in the butter with a pastry blender until mixture resembles coarse meal. Add the milk and slightly beaten egg. Stir with a fork until just blended. Remove the hot mixture from the oven. Drop topping mixture onto the hot filling, making 6 biscuits. Return the ramekins to the oven and bake until lightly browned, 15 to 20 minutes.

Whisk together the remaining ¼ cup sugar and cinnamon; sprinkle evenly over cobblers. Allow cobblers to cool 5 to 10 minutes before serving.

Notes: The recipe may be doubled to accommodate buffet service. Frozen unsweetened blueberries and peaches may be substituted if fresh fruit is unavailable. This recipe is also delicious with blackberries and peaches. Cobblers are best enjoyed warm from the oven.

Apple Walnut Streusel Cake with Cinnamon Custard

CAKE

1 cup corn oil

1½ cups sugar

4 eggs, beaten

2½ teaspoons vanilla extract

½ cup orange juice

3 cups all-purpose flour

3 teaspoons baking powder

STREUSEL AND FILLING

⅓ cup white sugar

¼ cup brown sugar

½ cup all-purpose flour

2 teaspoons cinnamon

½ cup coarsely chopped walnuts

2 tablespoons cold butter, cut into bits

3 large apples, peeled, cored and sliced

CUSTARD

1½ cups half-and-half

4 egg yolks

¼ cup sugar

2 teaspoons vanilla extract

3 teaspoons cinnamon

SERVES 6 TO 8

THIS IS A PERFECT "DO-AHEAD" CAKE FOR BREAKFAST or brunch, and the toasted leftovers make a fabulous addition to bread pudding.

CAKE: Preheat oven to 350° F. Combine oil and sugar. Add beaten eggs, vanilla and orange juice. Mix in flour and baking powder. Beat until just smooth.

STREUSEL: Mix the streusel ingredients together. Toss half the streusel with the apples to coat slightly.

In a well-greased and floured 14-cup tube pan, spread half the batter. Layer half the streusel mixture with all of the apple slices in the center. Spread the remaining batter over; sprinkle with the remaining streusel. Bake for 1 hour and 40 minutes or until a toothpick inserted in the middle comes out clean.

CUSTARD: While the cake is baking, scald the half-and-half in a medium saucepan. In a medium metal bowl, whisk together the egg yolks and sugar. Whisk the half-and-half into the egg mixture; whisk to combine well. Pour the mixture into a saucepan and cook over low heat until it just begins to thicken. Immediately pour the custard into a small metal bowl and submerge the bottom of the bowl into very cold water to stop it from cooking; whisk until cooled slightly. Whisk in the vanilla and cinnamon. Serve each piece of cake in a pool of warm custard sauce.

NOTES: Custard may be made up to 24 hours in advance and stored in the refrigerator in an airtight container. Rewarm over low heat before serving. The cake may be made up to 24 hours in advance.

Use slightly tart baking apples like McIntosh or Rome.

Blackberry Cream Streusel Cake with Cinnamon Cream

Cake Batter and Crumb Topping

- *2¼ cups all-purpose flour*
- *½ cup sugar*
- *¾ cup butter*
- *1 teaspoon baking powder*
- *1 teaspoon baking soda*
- *1 teaspoon salt*
- *¾ cup sour cream*
- *1 egg*
- *1 teaspoon almond extract*

Filling

- *8 oz. cream cheese*
- *¼ cup sour cream*
- *1 egg*
- *¼ cup sugar*
- *1 teaspoon almond extract*
- *1 cup seedless blackberry preserves*

Cinnamon Custard Cream

- *1 cup milk*
- *1 cup heavy cream*
- *4 egg yolks*
- *⅓ cup light brown sugar*
- *2 teaspoons cinnamon*

SERVES 6 TO 8

This is a wonderful cake to bake in the dead of winter—the blackberry preserves will bring back the sweet flavor of summer.

Cake and Topping: Preheat oven to 350° F; grease a 9- or 10-inch springform pan. In a large bowl, combine flour and sugar. With a pastry blender, cut in the butter until crumbly. Remove and reserve 1 cup of this crumb mixture. Add the baking powder, soda and salt and combine well. In a separate small bowl, whisk together the sour cream, egg and almond extract. Stir the sour cream mixture into the dry mixture and combine well. Pour the batter into the pan evenly.

Filling and Assembly: With an electric mixer, beat together the cream cheese, sour cream, egg and sugar. Mix in the almond extract. Spread the mixture over the batter; spoon the preserves evenly over the cheese mixture. Sprinkle the reserved crumb mixture over the top. Bake for 45 minutes, until firm and lightly browned.

Cinnamon Cream: In a medium saucepan, combine the milk and cream and cook over medium heat until just ready to boil. Remove from heat. In a medium mixing bowl, whisk together the egg yolks and light brown sugar until well combined. Pour the milk mixture into the egg mixture and whisk to combine well.

Prepare a large bowl with ice and water and a second smaller empty bowl for the custard. Return the mixture to the saucepan and cook over low heat, stirring constantly, until it just begins to thicken and coat the spoon. Immediately remove the mixture from the heat and pour it into the empty bowl. Submerge the bottom of the bowl in the ice water to stop the cooking and prevent overthickening, and stir until cooled slightly. Stir in the cinnamon. Refrigerate until serving. Serve each piece of cake on a pool of custard.

Notes: The cinnamon cream may be made up to 24 hours in advance and stored in the refrigerator.

The cake may be made up to 24 hours ahead and reheated for serving if desired.

Peach Streusel Coffeecake

Streusel Topping

- *⅓ cup all-purpose flour*
- *2 tablespoons butter, softened*
- *2 tablespoons light brown sugar*
- *½ teaspoon ground cinnamon*

Cake

- *1¼ cups all-purpose flour*
- *¼ cup granulated sugar*
- *1½ teaspoons baking powder*
- *½ teaspoon salt*
- *¼ cup butter*
- *¼ cup milk*
- *1 large egg*
- *½ teaspoon almond extract*
- *1 lb. fresh peaches, peeled, pitted and thinly sliced*

SERVES 6 TO 8

One of the great pleasures of summer in the country is the abundance of fresh produce. Without question, the peaches from Zimmerman's Orchard down the road are the sweetest, most luscious you will taste in your lifetime. I get excited just thinking about that first fuzzy bite and the sweet nectar running down my chin. Unlike those supermarket fruit "hardballs," these are the peaches you will remember from your childhood. Our local orchard has over fifty varieties—enough to keep us in juicy peaches from early July to mid-September.

Preheat oven to 400° F. Grease and flour a 9- or 10-inch springform pan.

Topping: Combine all the ingredients with a fork until crumbly; set aside.

Cake: Combine the flour, sugar, baking powder and salt. Cut in the butter with a pastry blender until it resembles coarse crumbs. Beat together the milk, egg and almond extract. Stir the milk mixture into the flour mixture until smooth. Spread the batter evenly in the prepared pan.

Assembly: Arrange the peach slices in an overlapping pattern on top and sprinkle evenly with the streusel.

Bake 35 to 40 minutes, or until the peaches are tender and a toothpick inserted into the cake comes out clean. Serve warm.

Notes: To prevent browning, drop sliced, peeled peaches into a bowl of cold water to which 2 to 3 tablespoons of lemon juice has been added.

Streusel ingredients may be prepared up to 12 hours ahead and stored covered in the refrigerator.

The cake is best served warm from the oven, but may be prepared up to 1 day in advance and reheated for serving.

Carrot, Pumpkin and Pecan Cakes with Orange Filling

Cakes

- ⅔ cup corn oil
- 1 cup sugar
- 1½ cups all-purpose flour
- 1 teaspoon cinnamon
- 1 teaspoon baking powder
- 1 teaspoon salt
- 2 eggs
- 2¼ cups grated carrots
- ¾ cup pumpkin purée (canned or homemade)
- ½ cup chopped pecans

Filling

- 1 cup mascarpone cheese
- ¼ cup sugar
- 3 tablespoons Grand Marnier
- 2 teaspoons orange juice
- ½ cup heavy cream

Glaze

- ½ cup confectioner's sugar
- 3 tablespoons butter, softened
- 2 tablespoons Grand Marnier
- 2 teaspoons orange juice
- 2 to 3 tablespoons hot water
- 1 tablespoon orange zest

SERVES 6

These individual cream cakes take the standard carrot cake a step further with the addition of pumpkin and a creamy orange filling.

Cakes: Preheat oven to 350° F. Grease and flour 6 1-cup individual bundtlette pans. Whisk together the corn oil and sugar. Sift together the flour, cinnamon, baking powder and salt. Add the dry mixture to the oil and sugar alternately with the eggs. Mix well. Add the carrots, pumpkin purée and pecans. Pour the batter into the prepared pans and bake for 50 minutes or until the cakes shrink slightly from the sides of the pans. Remove immediately from pans.

Filling: In a medium bowl, whisk together the mascarpone and sugar. Whisk in the Grand Marnier and orange juice. Whip the cream to soft peaks and gently fold it into the cheese mixture; refrigerate until ready to use.

Glaze: Whip together the butter and sugar. Whisk in the Grand Marnier and orange juice. Sprinkle in hot water until the mixture reaches the consistency of a glaze. Stir in the orange zest; keep warm.

Assembly: To serve, place the cakes on individual plates and fill the centers with the filling. Drizzle warm glaze over the tops.

Notes: A single large bundt pan or tube pan can be used in place of the bundtlette pans. However, the recipe must be doubled to fill a standard 12-cup pan and the baking time increased by 40 minutes. To fill, turn the cake over and hollow out a channel on the bottom.

To prepare fresh pumpkin purée: Choose a fresh "pie" pumpkin (generally smaller and less watery than carving pumpkins) and remove the stem and seeds. Cut the pumpkin into 1- to 2-inch chunks and steam over boiling water until tender, about 12 minutes. Allow to cool and remove rind. Purée remaining pulp in a food processor or blender. A 5-lb. pumpkin yields approximately 4 cups of purée. Any unused portion may be frozen for up to 3 months in sealed containers for later use.

Canned pumpkin purée may be substituted for the fresh purée if necessary. The filling may be made up to 24 hours in advance. The cakes may be frozen, well-wrapped, for up to 2 weeks or baked the day before serving.

Lemon Poppy Seed Sandwiches with Lemon Cream Filling

Loaf

6 tablespoons butter
6 tablespoons shortening
1 cup sugar
2 eggs
¾ cup milk
4 tablespoons lemon juice
3 cups all-purpose flour
2 teaspoons baking powder
1 teaspoon salt
¼ cup poppy seeds

Filling

1 cup mascarpone cheese
½ cup sugar
¼ cup lemon juice
½ cup heavy cream

Assembly

¼ cup confectioner's sugar for dusting

MAKES 18 SMALL SANDWICHES

Delicious for a picnic breakfast and equally at home on the finest china, these elegant little "sandwiches" have a creamy mascarpone filling scented with lemon. Save leftovers as a delicious snack with afternoon tea.

Loaf: Preheat oven to 350° F. Grease a 9 × 5-inch loaf pan.

Cream together the butter, shortening and sugar. Beat together eggs, milk and lemon juice. Mix together flour, baking powder and salt. Alternately add the wet ingredients and the dry to the butter-sugar mixture. Stir in the poppy seeds. Spread the batter in the prepared loaf pan. Bake for 55 minutes or until a toothpick inserted into the loaf comes out clean. Allow to cool thoroughly. Cut into approximately 18 ½-inch thick slices.

Filling: In a medium bowl or with an electric mixer, whisk together the mascarpone and sugar until smooth. Stir in the lemon juice. Whip the cream to soft peaks and fold it into the mascarpone mixture.

Assembly: Spread a slice of poppy seed loaf with cream filling and top with another slice, making a small sandwich. Repeat until all slices are used. Cut sandwiches in half, dust with confectioner's sugar, and serve.

Notes: This bread may be frozen (unfilled) for up to 1 month and defrosted before serving. The filling may be made up to 24 hours in advance. Sandwiches may be assembled up to 24 hours ahead and kept under refrigeration (or in a cooler) until serving.

Baked Apple with Oatmeal, Cinnamon and Pecans in Phyllo

4 apples, preferably McIntosh or Rome

2 tablespoons brown sugar

1 teaspoon cinnamon

4 tablespoons uncooked, old-fashioned oatmeal

¼ cup chopped pecans (optional)

2 tablespoons butter

4 sheets phyllo dough

½ cup melted butter or no-stick baking spray oil

SERVES 4

THIS UNIQUE VERSION OF A BAKED APPLE WILL HEIGHTEN your guests' anticipation of what's to follow. It also makes a delicious low-fat baked treat.

Preheat oven to 375° F. Lightly grease a baking sheet.

Keep phyllo dough covered until ready to use. Core the apples and peel 1 inch of skin from around the tops. Mix together the brown sugar, cinnamon, oatmeal and pecans. Place the apples upright in an ungreased 9 × 12-inch glass baking dish. Spoon the oatmeal mixture into the centers of the apples, dividing evenly. Dot the center of each apple with ½ tablespoon butter. Pour hot water ¼ inch deep into the baking dish. Bake uncovered until slightly tender, about 20 minutes.

Remove the pan from the oven; carefully remove the apples and place them on paper towels. Lay out one sheet of phyllo and brush lightly with melted butter or spray with no-stick spray. Set the next sheet on top and repeat until all 4 layers have been prepared. With a sharp knife, cut the phyllo into 4 squares. Place each cooked apple in the middle of a layered square. Bring two opposite corners of pastry squares up over each apple and pinch together. Repeat with the other corners and crimp the edges. Brush any remaining butter on the outside of the apple packages and place them on the baking sheet. Bake for 7 minutes or until the pastry is lightly browned and crisp. Serve warm.

NOTES: Phyllo pastry can be purchased from the freezer section of the grocery store and is subject to the hazards of freezer storage. The leaves may become brittle from freezer burn and may clump together from thawing and subsequent refreezing. Since there is no way to tell how fresh phyllo leaves are without opening the package, I suggest buying them from a busy grocery or gourmet shop that regularly rotates its stock and has several packages on hand. If, upon opening, the leaves are brittle or clumped, discard them and open a fresh package. Once the package is opened, the leaves will dry out quickly; cover the unused leaves with a slightly damp towel and work quickly. The assembled items should be covered with plastic until all are completed. If not baking immediately, wrap the items tightly with plastic wrap and store in the refrigerator.

Creamy Arborio Rice Pudding with Amaretto and Caramelized Sugar

1 cup arborio rice
4 cups half-and-half
1 cup milk
⅓ cup sugar
1 teaspoon almond extract
½ cup golden raisins
2 large egg yolks
1 cup heavy cream
4 tablespoons amaretto
2 teaspoons freshly grated nutmeg
¼ cup sugar

SERVES 6 TO 8

Rice pudding is a fabulous alternative to flour-based baked goods. Arborio is the short-grained Italian rice used to make risotto. If you're as big a fan of risotto as I am, you'll realize that that creamy quality makes for an outstanding rice pudding. Add a hint of Amaretto and a crisp sugar top, and it's quite heavenly.

Combine the rice, half-and-half, milk, sugar, almond extract, and raisins in a large saucepan. Simmer over low heat, stirring constantly, for about 30 minutes or until tender. Briskly stir in the egg yolks and cook for 4 to 5 more minutes until thickened. Stir in the cream and amaretto and cool at room temperature.

When ready to serve, preheat the broiler. Spoon the pudding into a small (9 × 5-inch) ovenproof glass pan or individual ramekins and smooth the top. Sprinkle with nutmeg and sift on the sugar. Place the pudding under the broiler for 2 to 4 minutes, just until the sugar caramelizes (it will turn light brown). Quickly remove from the broiler to avoid burning, cool for 1 minute, and serve immediately.

NOTES: A small propane torch (the kind plumbers use) is a convenient tool for creating the crisp sugar top known as brûlée. It's the method favored by many professional pastry chefs. For a special treat, try the crisp topping on a shallow bowl of creamy oatmeal. First top the oatmeal with a little heavy cream, then sprinkle on the sugar.

The pudding may be made up to 48 hours in advance before caramelizing and stored, tightly covered, in the refrigerator. Bring to room temperature before caramelizing. The caramelized topping will hold for only 5 to 10 minutes, so serve the pudding immediately. Humidity will affect how long the topping stays crisp.

2.75
2.75

Beverages, Fruits and Soups for Starters

Our breakfast menus offer a balance of healthful eating—a fresh fruit dish, fresh fruit juice and sometimes even a fruity or savory soup. Soup for breakfast—sounds absurd? The idea for serving a small cup of savory soup for breakfast came from a friend, who sometimes takes the leftover soup home from our Saturday night dinners. She often remarks how wonderful it tastes the next morning in lieu of cereal—and why not? These soups share many of the ingredients typically used in omelettes or quiches. Warm-from-the-oven baked goods and a positively decadent entrée complete the meal.

Guests often ask us whether we ever go out for breakfasts like these, and our answer is that we never eat breakfasts like these—where would we find them? Most guests skip lunch after a Twin Linden breakfast and swear off eating forever—or at least until they return for afternoon tea.

Cinnamon Nutmeg Eggnog

—

Gazpacho Tomato Juice Cocktail

—

Cinnamon Peach Nectar

—

Strawberry Pear Frothy

—

Orange Peach Iced Tea

—

Cranberry Grapefruit Cocktail

—

Strawberry Lemon Spritzer

—

Capuccino Hot Chocolate

—

White Grape Juice Cocktail

—

Strawberries, Bananas and Strawberry Mint Coulis

—

Pineapple with Blackberry, Figs and Lemon

—

Sliced Apple with Raisins, Walnuts and Honey Poppy Seed Glaze

—

Sweet Honeydew with Berries and Blueberry Banana Sauce

—

Lemon Poached Pears with Berry Pear Sauce

—

Cantaloupe with Blackberry Peach Purée

—

Orange, Kiwi and Banana Slices with Orange Honey Glaze

—

Strawberry Champagne Soup

—

Cantaloupe Soup with Blackberry Swirl

—

Artichoke Dill Soup

—

White Seafood Gazpacho

—

Broccoli Roquefort Soup

—

Roasted Garlic Soup with Roasted Yellow Pepper Crème Fraîche

—

Wild Mushroom and Pancetta Soup

Cinnamon Nutmeg Eggnog

Custard

3 egg yolks

⅓ cup sugar

2½ cups milk

2½ cups half-and-half

1 teaspoon vanilla extract

1 teaspoon cinnamon

½ teaspoon freshly grated nutmeg

Meringue and Cream

½ cup sugar

½ cup corn syrup

½ cup water

6 egg whites

1 cup heavy cream

1 cup milk

Assembly

Freshly ground nutmeg

SERVES 6 TO 8

The challenge of making eggnog without using raw eggs resulted in this creamy holiday drink. Italian meringue is a cooked version of the traditional whipped meringue. Although it involves a little more preparation, it has the added bonus of greater stability than raw meringue.

Custard: In a medium saucepan, whisk together egg yolks and sugar. Stir in the milk. Cook over low heat until mixture coats a spoon, 3 to 4 minutes. Remove from heat and stir in the half-and-half. Stir in the vanilla, cinnamon and nutmeg. Cool to room temperature and refrigerate for at least 2 hours.

Meringue and Cream: In a small saucepan, combine sugar, corn syrup and water. Bring to a boil and cook until the mixture reaches the soft-ball stage (240° F on a candy thermometer), about 5 minutes. Remove from heat and set aside. In a large bowl of an electric mixer, whisk egg whites until soft peaks form. With mixer running, gradually pour the hot syrup into the egg whites. Continue beating egg whites until cool and stiff, about 5 minutes.

Assembly: To serve, pour the custard into a large bowl. Fold in the meringue until combined but with some peaks still showing. Stir in the heavy cream and milk. Divide among glasses and serve with freshly ground nutmeg.

Gazpacho Tomato Juice Cocktail

2 tablespoons lemon juice
2 roasted red bell peppers, seeded and chopped
¼ cup chopped onion
1 teaspoon chopped jalapeño pepper
2 cups tomato juice
½ teaspoon coarsely ground pepper
1 tablespoon finely grated or prepared horseradish
4 scallions, tips removed (optional)

SERVES 4 TO 6

THE FLAVORFUL INGREDIENTS OF TRADITIONAL GAZPACHO are natural enhancers for tomato juice and make a terrific base for a Bloody Mary.

In a food processor or blender, combine the lemon juice, peppers, onion and jalapeño and process until just blended but not puréed. Add the tomato juice, about ½ cup at a time, until blended. Stir in the ground pepper and horseradish, garnish with scallions and serve cold.

Cinnamon Peach Nectar

1 cup peeled and sliced fresh peaches (about 2 large)
2 tablespoons sugar
2 teaspoons cinnamon
3 tablespoons lemon juice
1½ cups canned peach nectar

SERVES 4 TO 6

THIS IS THE EQUIVALENT OF DRINKING A PEACH PIE— fabulously decadent but also naturally low in fat.

Toss together the peaches, sugar, cinnamon and lemon juice. In a food processor or blender, combine the peaches and peach nectar and process until smooth. Serve cold.

Strawberry Pear Frothy

4 cups fresh ripe strawberries, hulled and quartered (about 2 qts.)
2 ripe pears, peeled, cored and sliced
1 cup plain low- or nonfat yogurt
½ cup fresh orange juice
Mint leaves, additional strawberries or orange slices (optional)

SERVES 4

FRESH LOCAL STRAWBERRIES ARE ONE OF THE REAL JOYS of country life. These varieties are chosen for their sweetness, not for their ability to withstand rough cross-country shipping. A deep red color all the way through, local berries provide the basis for many of our springtime fruit dishes and desserts. This smooth fruit drink incorporates the sweet berry flavor with the tang of creamy yogurt.

Combine berries, pears, yogurt and orange juice in a blender and process until smooth. Garnish with fresh mint, strawberries or orange slices if desired.

NOTE: May be made up to 1 day ahead and kept under refrigeration until ready to serve.

Orange Peach Iced Tea

1½ cups peeled, pitted and sliced peaches (about 4 large)
¼ cup sugar
2 tablespoons lemon juice
5 cups cold water
4 tea bags
½ cup fresh orange juice

SERVES 4 TO 6

THE EARLY HEAT OF WARM SUMMER DAYS CALLS FOR A cool icy version of morning tea.

In a medium bowl, toss together the peaches, sugar and lemon juice; set aside. In a medium saucepan, bring the water to a boil. Add the tea bags and set aside to steep. Cool to room temperature. In a blender or food processor, combine the orange juice and peaches and process until puréed. Add 2 cups of the tea and process again. Pour the remaining tea into a large pitcher and stir in the orange-peach purée. Serve cold.

FOLLOWING PAGES: *Cinnamon Peach Nectar; Strawberry Lemon Spritzer; White Grape Juice Cocktail; Orange Peach Iced Tea; Strawberry Pear Frothy*

Cranberry Grapefruit Cocktail

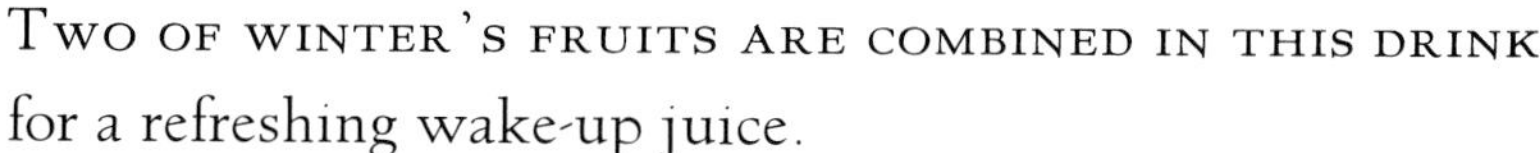

Two of winter's fruits are combined in this drink for a refreshing wake-up juice.

2 cups fresh cranberries
¼ cup sugar
2 tablespoons water
1½ cups fresh grapefruit juice

SERVES 4 TO 6

In a medium saucepan, combine cranberries, sugar and water. Bring to a boil, then lower heat and simmer, stirring constantly, until cranberries "pop," about 5 minutes. Cool to room temperature. With a food mill or sieve, press cranberries to collect juice and pulp and to remove skins. Combine cranberry and grapefruit juice in a blender and whiz until smooth. Serve cold.

Note: May be made up to 24 hours in advance.

Strawberry Lemon Spritzer

During the postholiday "blahs," everybody seems to be on a diet, but innkeeping resumes full swing in February, with Valentine's Day. It has become so popular an occasion that we run our Valentine's Package every weekend through February. With it comes the need for extra-special menus and elaborate breakfast items, often in shades of red or pink. This drink is best made with fresh strawberries, but frozen ones will adapt to this recipe well and provide the perfect pink beverage. You may need to adjust for sweetness by adding sugar if the strawberries are frozen or less than fully ripe.

2 cups fresh ripe strawberries, hulled and quartered
3 teaspoons lemon juice
1 qt. club soda
Lemon wedges (optional)
Mint leaves (optional)

SERVES 4 TO 6

Combine strawberries and lemon juice in a food processor or blender and process until smooth. Stir in club soda, garnish with lemon wedges and mint and serve.

Capuccino Hot Chocolate

6 oz. fine semi-sweet chocolate
4 cups milk
1 teaspoon instant coffee
4 tablespoons Grand Marnier (optional)
4 tablespoons Tía María (optional)
4 cinnamon sticks

SERVES 4 TO 6

IN LIEU OF FRESHLY GROUND COFFEE, A SPECIAL WINTER morning might warrant frothy hot cocoa with steam-infused milk. Add a little Grand Marnier and Tía María for extra-rich flavor, and let it snow.

Coarsely chop the chocolate. In a medium saucepan, heat 3 cups of the milk and the chocolate, stirring until chocolate is melted and mixture is ready to come to a boil. Add instant coffee and stir well; stir in the liqueurs.

If you have an espresso machine, follow the manufacturer's instructions to froth the remaining 1 cup milk. Or, bring the milk to a boil, then whip in a blender for 2 minutes. Pour chocolate mixture into 4 warm mugs and spoon on frothy milk. Serve garnished with cinnamon sticks.

NOTE: The hot chocolate may be made without the frothy milk, cooled and refrigerated for up to 1 day in advance.

White Grape Juice Cocktail

2 cups white grape juice
¼ cup grapefruit juice
1 8-oz. bottle club soda

SERVES 4 TO 6

WHILE A GREAT BOTTLE OF WINE WOULD ADD A MELLOW mood to a late-morning brunch, a tasty nonalcoholic substitute might be a classic wine spritzer, sans the wine. Here, I've used white grape juice.

Simply combine juices and soda. Serve chilled.

Strawberries, Bananas and Strawberry Mint Coulis

Coulis

- 1 cup strawberries, hulled and quartered
- 10 fresh mint leaves
- 2 tablespoons lemon juice
- 2 tablespoons sugar (optional)

Assembly

- 2 large bananas, peeled
- 1 cup strawberries, hulled and sliced
- 4 mint sprigs
- 1 teaspoon lemon zest
- Edible flowers (optional)

SERVES 4

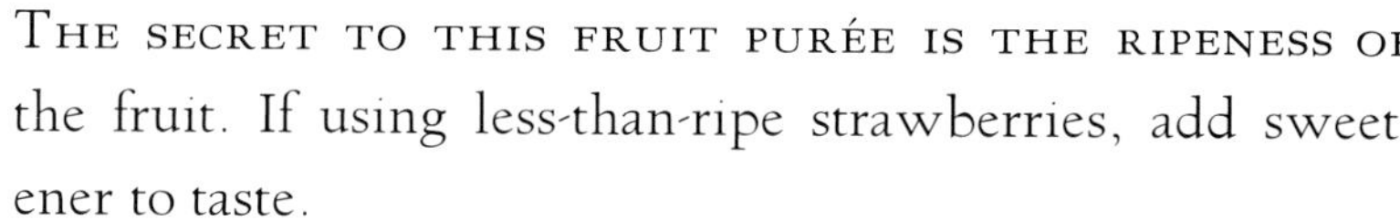

The secret to this fruit purée is the ripeness of the fruit. If using less-than-ripe strawberries, add sweetener to taste.

Mint is a wonderful herb for enhancing fruit and for garnishing, but beware planting any variety among your herbs—it is extremely intrusive and will take over in no time. Instead, find a separate area for the mint in well-tilled soil and let it roam where it may. After it takes hold, you'll never have a shortage.

Coulis: In a small bowl, toss the strawberries and mint leaves; refrigerate for 1 hour. Remove and discard the mint leaves. In a blender or food processor, combine strawberries, lemon juice and sugar and process until smooth. Refrigerate until ready to use.

Assembly: Cut bananas in half. Cut each piece lengthwise in quarters. Arrange pieces on 4 individual plates. Divide strawberries among the plates, arranged on one side of the bananas. Spoon the coulis on the other side of the bananas. Garnish with the mint, lemon zest and flowers.

Notes: Edible flowers make a beautiful addition to any presentation and are particularly lovely on fresh fruit dishes and salads. The fact that the flowers are edible makes them acceptable enhancements for food, but it doesn't mean that you have to eat them. One of our less-impressed breakfast guests once described the taste of a pansy as being similar (or so he imagined) to that of facial tissue, but many people attribute particular flavors to different blooms.

In the summer, I grow a large garden filled with nasturtiums and pansies to supply me with beautiful edible flowers till the late October frost. I also often use herb blossoms (chives, sage and thyme) to enhance the presentation of savory dishes.

Pineapple with Blackberry, Figs and Lemon

- 1 small ripe pineapple
- 1 cup blackberries
- ½ cup strawberries, hulled and quartered
- 2 teaspoons lemon juice
- 2 tablespoons sugar
- 4 ripe figs, quartered
- 12 additional blackberries
- 1 teaspoon lemon zest

SERVES 4

If fresh figs are unavailable, add the fig flavor by sprinkling some chopped dried figs over the fresh pineapple.

Cut off the top and bottom of the pineapple. Slice off the skin and remove any eyes. Cut the pineapple into 4 1-inch rings; remove the hard core from each ring. Combine 1 cup blackberries with the strawberries, lemon juice and sugar in a food processor or blender and purée.

To serve, place pineapple slices on 4 individual plates. Arrange 4 pieces of fig in the center of each. Spoon purée on the side and place 3 blackberries on each plate. Garnish with lemon zest.

Sliced Apple with Raisins, Walnuts and Honey Poppy Seed Glaze

4 medium slightly tart apples (Rome, Granny Smith or McIntosh)

4 teaspoons lemon juice

¼ cup honey

2 teaspoons poppy seeds

2 teaspoons lemon zest

¼ cup walnut pieces

¼ cup golden raisins

SERVES 4

This is a simple fruit dish that contrasts nicely with some of the sweet (as opposed to savory) main entrées. Our fruit dishes are most often fresh, to emphasize the natural sweetness of the fruit. In this case, the honey glaze provides a counterpoint to the tartness of the apples. If you prefer to serve a warm cooked dish, the glazed apple slices may be heated in a microwave oven for 60 seconds on high or until slightly soft.

Core apples and slice into ¼-inch pieces. Toss in 2 teaspoons lemon juice to prevent browning. Combine the honey, poppy seeds, remaining lemon juice and zest to make a glaze; coat the apple slices with the glaze. Arrange the slices in a fan shape on individual chilled salad dishes. Sprinkle with the walnuts and raisins, spoon on any additional glaze and serve.

Sweet Honeydew with Berries and Blueberry Banana Sauce

- *1 ripe honeydew, halved, seeds removed*
- *1 cup blueberries*
- *1 ripe banana, peeled and quartered*
- *2 tablespoons orange juice*
- *1 teaspoon lemon juice*
- *2 tablespoons sugar, or to taste*
- *½ cup firm ripe raspberries*
- *Sprigs of mint and edible flowers like pansies*

SERVES 4

OUR FRESH FRUIT PURÉES ARE TO OUR MORNING FRUIT dishes as stock is to our soups—much of their flavor comes from combining the wonderful trimmings that are not otherwise usable because of their appearance.

In their season—late summer—we use local melons almost exclusively. They tend to be riper and sweeter than commercially-grown ones because they stay longer on the vine. The honeydew melons we get have a webbed, not smooth skin, but their inside color and texture are the same.

Cut 8½-inch slices from the honeydew and remove the rind. (Keep the remaining melon for another use.) In a blender or food processor, combine the blueberries, banana, orange juice, lemon juice and sugar; process until smooth. Arrange 2 slices of honeydew, touching at one end, on each of 4 individual plates and pour ¼ cup sauce onto one side. Sprinkle raspberries over and garnish with mint and/or flowers.

NOTES: When creating your own purées, use these general rules to guide you: (1) use only firm ripe trimmings—soft spots should be discarded; (2) avoid fruits that contain a lot of liquid or fiber, like pineapple or apple—they will dilute the flavor; (3) add banana for a thicker purée; (4) add a few tablespoons of fresh fruit juice like lemon or orange for a smoother blend; (5) use a blender rather than a food processor to incorporate more air into the blend and make it frothier.

Lemon Poached Pears with Berry Pear Sauce

Sauce

1 cup raspberries

½ cup blackberries

1 cup strawberries, hulled and quartered

2 ripe pears, peeled, cored and quartered

4 tablespoons fresh orange juice

2 tablespoons raspberry liqueur, such as Chambord (optional)

Pears

4 cups water

½ cup sugar

3 teaspoons lemon juice

2 teaspoons lemon zest

4 medium firm pears, peeled and cored

Assembly

Additional lemon zest

SERVES 4

Using ripe pears and sweet berries will enhance this dessert with a delicate natural sweetness. This dish is inherently low in fat and calories, but the taste won't give it away.

Sauce: Combine the ingredients in a food processor or blender and process until smooth. Refrigerate until ready to serve.

Pears: In a large saucepan, combine the water, sugar, lemon juice and zest. Bring the liquid to a boil. Reduce to a simmer and add the pears. Poach pears for 10 to 12 minutes or until tender when pierced with the point of a sharp knife. Remove the pears from the liquid and cool slightly. Refrigerate pears in liquid until serving time (may be done overnight).

Assembly: To serve, spoon pools of purée onto 4 individual plates. Stand the pears upright in the sauce and spoon remaining sauce on top. Garnish with lemon zest.

Note: The pears can be poached up to 2 days in advance. The sauce can be made 24 hours in advance.

Opposite: *Orange, Kiwi and Banana Slices with Orange Honey Glaze; Lemon Poached Pears with Berry Pear Sauce; Cantaloupe with Blackberry Peach Puree*

Cantaloupe with Blackberry Peach Purée

1 ripe cantaloupe, halved, seeds removed
1 cup blackberries
2 medium-ripe peaches, peeled, pitted and quartered
2 tablespoons lemon juice
2 tablespoons sugar, or to taste
12 firm blackberries
½ cup blueberries
Mint sprigs and edible flowers

SERVES 4

THIS PURÉE MAKES A TERRIFIC LOW-CAL SAUCE FOR pancakes or French toast. Other varieties of melon, such as the ones we are beginning to see in our markets from Israel and France also are good in this dish.

Cut 8½-inch slices from the cantaloupe and remove the rind. (Keep the remaining melon for another use.) In a blender or food processor, combine the blackberries, peaches, lemon juice, and sugar; process until smooth. Arrange 2 slices of cantaloupe next to each other on 4 individual plates and pour ¼ cup purée across the middle. Sprinkle blackberries and blueberries over top and garnish with the mint and/or flowers.

Orange, Kiwi and Banana Slices with Orange Honey Glaze

¼ cup fresh orange juice
2 tablespoons honey
3 medium oranges
2 ripe kiwi
2 large firm bananas

SERVES 4

Once, in the deep of winter, I wandered down the produce aisle of the local market looking for any variety of truly fresh fruit. What I saw before me was a barren wasteland. And so, borne of necessity, here is a fruit dish that utilizes the only three decent fruits available on a cold winter day. This delicious combination might make you forget for a moment your longing for fresh summer bounty.

In a small bowl, whisk together the orange juice and honey; set aside. Peel the oranges and cut each into 8 wedges. Peel the kiwi and cut into ¼-inch-thick slices. Peel bananas and cut into ¼-inch slices. Place 3 slices of kiwi in the center of each of 4 plates. Arrange the banana slices around the kiwi. Arrange orange wedges in a circular pattern over kiwi and bananas. Use a pastry brush to glaze with the orange-honey mixture and serve.

Strawberry Champagne Soup

- 4 cups fresh strawberries, hulled and quartered
- 1 cup orange juice
- 2 tablespoons orange brandy (like Grand Marnier)
- 2 tablespoons sugar, or to taste
- ¾ cup crème fraîche
- 1 cup dry champagne

SERVES 4 TO 6

THIS SOUP IS DESIGNED FOR APPEARANCE AS WELL AS taste to enhance a romantic early summer breakfast.

In a food processor or blender, combine strawberries, orange juice, brandy and sugar; process until smooth. Pour into a medium bowl and whisk in the crème fraîche. Chill for 30 minutes. Stir in the champagne just before serving.

NOTES: A wonderful cream mixture that won't curdle in sauces, crème fraîche can be purchased or made at home. Whisk together equal portions of sour cream and heavy cream. Cover with plastic and allow to ripen at room temperature for 12 hours. The mixture will thicken. Refrigerate thoroughly before using. Crème fraîche is also the perfect foil to ripe fresh berries for a simple dessert.

The soup may be made without adding the champagne up to 24 hours in advance. Club soda is a nonalcoholic alternative to the champagne.

Cantaloupe Soup with Blackberry Swirl

2 medium ripe cantaloupes, halved and seeded
3 tablespoons orange juice
1 cup low-fat plain yogurt
2 teaspoons lemon juice
1 cup blackberries
2 tablespoons honey

SERVES 6

Sometimes in the business of everyday life, I forget how lucky we are to live in such a productive farm area. A terrific reminder comes in late summer, when there are so many cantaloupes on the vine that they cost as little as 10 cents each. I know this is hard to believe, but it's absolutely true. And the old adage of "you get what you pay for" rings hollow when you scoop out that first juicy bite. That same sweet cantaloupe flavor makes a delicious base for soup, enlivened with a dark purple swirl of blackberries.

Remove the rind from the cantaloupe and cut the fruit into chunks. In a food processor or blender, combine the cantaloupe and orange juice and process until smooth. Add the yogurt and process just to combine; set aside.

In a food processor or blender, process the lemon juice and blackberries until smooth. Strain to remove any seeds and stir in the honey. Serve the soup cold topped with a swirl of the blackberry purée.

Artichoke Dill Soup

6 tablespoons lemon juice
3 cups low- or nonfat plain yogurt
1½ cups chicken stock
½ cup crème fraîche
¼ cup chopped fresh dill
2 teaspoons ground white pepper
Dill sprigs
18 cooked artichoke hearts or store-bought marinated artichoke hearts, drained
Additional artichoke hearts, chopped

SERVES 6 TO 8

If fresh ones aren't available, use marinated artichoke hearts, which will add a savory seasoning to this soup. Make the soup a day ahead to allow the flavors to fully develop.

Coarsely chop the artichoke hearts and toss them in a large bowl with lemon juice. Add the yogurt, chicken stock, crème fraîche, dill and pepper and stir well. Transfer mixture to a food processor and process until smooth. Remove to another bowl, cover and chill for at least 2 hours. Correct seasoning to taste and garnish with dill sprigs and the chopped artichoke hearts before serving.

White Seafood Gazpacho

- *¼ cup dry white wine*
- *1 cup water*
- *1½ lbs. sea scallops*
- *2 lbs. plain low-fat yogurt*
- *1 lb. sour cream*
- *1½ cups heavy cream*
- *2 teaspoons white pepper*
- *¼ teaspoon cayenne pepper*
- *1 cup bottled clam juice*
- *1 jalapeño pepper, seeded and sliced*
- *1 green bell pepper, seeded and sliced*
- *1 lb. large shrimp, cooked, peeled and deveined*
- *1 lb. jumbo lump crab*
- *6 scallions, finely chopped*

SERVES 6 TO 8

THIS FABULOUS SAVORY COLD SOUP IS PERFECT FOR A warm summer morning. The smooth cool white appearance reveals little of the creamy seafood delight within.

Combine wine and water in a covered sauté pan and bring to a boil. Lower heat, add the scallops and cover. Cook the scallops until just done, 2 to 5 minutes, depending on their size. Remove the scallops and reserve the poaching liquid; cool thoroughly, then refrigerate scallops and liquid.

Combine yogurt, sour cream and heavy cream. Add white and cayenne peppers, clam juice and cooled poaching liquid. In a food processor or blender, combine about a cup of the mixture with the jalapeño and bell pepper strips and process until just specks of pepper are visible; fold into the remaining mixture. Again in a food processor or blender, whiz about a cup of the mixture with ⅓ lb. of the scallops and 6 shrimp until smooth; return to the mixture. Break the remaining seafood into bite-size pieces and fold into the mixture with the scallions. Chill well and serve.

NOTES: I sometimes substitute pieces of lobster for the scallops for an especially elegant dish.

Chill the serving bowls for at least 1 hour in the freezer to help maintain the temperature of the soup.

Broccoli Roquefort Soup

4 cups fresh broccoli florets
½ cup butter
1¼ cups finely chopped Vidalia (or other sweet) onions
¼ cup all-purpose flour
3 cups defatted chicken stock
2 cups half-and-half
1½ teaspoons ground white pepper
1 tablespoon Colman's dry mustard
1½ cup crumbled Roquefort

SERVES 6 TO 8

DON'T TURN THAT PAGE—FOR ALL YOU SKEPTICS, THIS unusual combination works. Fresh broccoli is one of the last vegetables of our growing season, appearing in the cool of autumn on the farmstands along with pumpkins and apple cider. Combined with imported French Roquefort, it makes a flavorful soup.

Blanch the broccoli florets: drop into boiling water for about 3 minutes or until just cooked, then immediately into a bowl of cold water; the florets should be bright green. Drain and set aside.

On low heat, melt the butter in a large saucepan, add onions, and sauté until tender and translucent (about 2 minutes). On medium heat, whisk in the flour and cook about 2 minutes. Whisking hard, add the chicken stock and half-and-half. Remove 1 cup of the mixture and set aside; bring the remainder to a boil. Purée the broccoli with the reserved cup of liquid in a food processor or blender. Stir this broccoli cream mixture into the soup base and heat just to a boil; remove from heat. Whisk in the pepper and dry mustard and cool for about 10 minutes. Add the crumbled Roquefort and stir to combine. Serve warm.

NOTE: Blanching is a way to fix the green color of vegetables and to guard against overcooking. Simply submerge the vegetables in boiling water. Cooking times can vary from an instant for snow peas and baby asparagus to up to 2 minutes for thicker asparagus spears or green beans—they should just turn bright green. Immediately immerse the vegetables in ice water to stop the cooking. They should be crisp and slightly undercooked, since they will finish cooking in their final preparation.

Roasted Garlic Soup with Yellow Pepper Crème Fraîche

- *8 heads of garlic, peeled and separated*
- *5 cups chicken stock*
- *3 tablespoons butter*
- *½ cup chopped onion*
- *3 tablespoons flour*
- *2 cups half-and-half*
- *2 teaspoons coarsely ground black pepper*
- *4 yellow peppers, roasted, peeled and seeded*
- *½ cup crème fraîche*

SERVES 6 TO 8

A BEAUTIFUL PRESENTATION AND A DELICIOUS CLASSIC combination of flavors make this soup ideal for special morning occasions.

Preheat oven to 400° F. Place the garlic in a shallow baking dish and pour in 1 cup of chicken stock. Cover with foil and roast for 1 hour; allow to cool slightly. Spoon the garlic and juices into a blender or food processor. Add another cup of chicken stock and process until smooth.

In a medium saucepan, melt the butter. Add the onion and sauté on low heat until translucent, about 2 minutes. Whisk in the flour and cook for 1 minute. Add the remaining 3 cups of chicken stock and whisk to combine; whisk in the garlic mixture. Add the half-and-half and bring just to a boil. Remove from heat, stir in the black pepper and allow to cool slightly.

In a food processor or blender, purée the yellow peppers until smooth. Add the crème fraîche and whiz just to combine. Serve soup topped with a swirl of the yellow pepper cream.

NOTE: The soup and yellow pepper cream may be made the night before and reheated, but swirl in the cream just before serving for a dramatic effect.

Wild Mushroom and Pancetta Soup

4 cups chopped shiitake and other wild mushrooms
1 cup heavy cream
¼ cup butter
1 cup finely chopped onion
3 tablespoons flour
4 cups chicken stock
2 cups half-and-half
2 tablespoons veal glacé
2 teaspoons ground white pepper
1 cup crumbled sautéed pancetta
½ cup Madeira
½ cup crème fraîche

SERVES 6 TO 8

WE LIVE NEAR KENNETT SQUARE, PENNSYLVANIA, THE self-proclaimed "Mushroom Capital of the World," which gives us great access to fresh varieties of mushrooms. The most widely available is the shiitake, and honestly, I don't think of it as "wild" or exotic because it has become my staple mushroom. It is deeply flavorful, and blended with a little veal stock and sherry, it provides a rich base for an exceptional mushroom soup.

In a food processor or blender, process the mushrooms with the heavy cream until whipped into a purée. Melt the butter in a large saucepan. Add the onions and sauté over medium heat until translucent. Whisk in the flour and cook for 2 minutes. Whisk in the chicken stock and half-and-half. Whisk in the mushroom mixture and bring just to a boil. Remove from heat and stir in veal glacé, white pepper and pancetta. Cool slightly.

Whisk together Madeira and crème fraîche; swirl the mixture into soup (this can be done in the shape of a mushroom) and serve.

NOTES: Summerfield Farms in Virginia is a good mail-order source of natural veal products, including its *eau de veau* (veal glacé), a reduced veal stock, which is invaluable as a flavor-enhancer and sauce base. Other brands may be found in the freezer section of a specialty food store.

The soup may be made up to 24 hours in advance and stored in the refrigerator until ready to serve.

Some soups, like consommés, are inherently low-fat, but cream soups present a real challenge for the fat conscious. Of course, one option in reducing your overall fat intake is to just eat less of a good thing by reducing the serving size. Another approach for lowering the fat content in a hot cream soup is to substitute 2% milk for some or all of the cream and half-and-half. This will water it down a lot, but you can add some thickness by puréeing 2 cups of cooked white rice with ¼ cup of milk or stock. Since fat is a flavor enhancer, the lower fat version may require more seasoning as well.

Exceptional Eggs

So perhaps you don't like eggs. You might like to know that many of the people who join us for breakfast preface their meal with this same assertion. Many others end their meal with a very different sentiment, as in "I usually don't like eggs, but . . ." Put aside your preconceptions and prejudices and take a fresh look at eggs from a unique perspective.

In the recipes that follow, I have generally omitted the addition of salt except where necessary for a baking reaction to occur, and I've used unsalted butter even if not specified. While I feel these dishes don't require the addition of salt, I also realize (since I live with a perfectly fit salt "fiend") that the addition of salt is often a matter of personal taste and health. So feel free to add salt as desired.

Pesto Eggs with Leeks and Asparagus

Tarragon-Baked Eggs in Brioche with Wild Mushrooms and Madeira

Crab, Egg and Brie Soufflés with Chive Sauce

Nested Eggs with Potato Blini, Chive Cream and Caviar

Egg Strata with Roasted Garlic, Tomatoes and Eggplant

Baked Eggs with Pancetta on Shredded Potato Nests

Eggs with Salmon in Dill Crêpes

Truffled Risotto Eggs with Spinach and Shaved Parmesan

Eggs "Oscar" with Lobster, Asparagus Tips and Tarragon Rounds

Cilantro Corn Pudding with Scallions, Peppers and Monterey Jack Cheese

Baked Eggs with Basil Pancakes and Plum Tomato Confit

Rolled Basil Soufflé with Roasted Red Pepper Coulis

Basil Crêpes with Ricotta, Eggs, Onions and Artichokes

Asparagus, Chèvre and Roasted Pepper Napoleon
with Pepper Cream

Smoked Trout Frittata

Wild Rice and Scallion Egg Tarts in Herb Crust

Asparagus Egg Tart with Roquefort, White Wine and Cracked Pepper

Crisp Noodle Cakes with Shrimp, Chinese Black Beans and Poached Eggs

Spring Rolls with Wild Mushrooms, Goat Cheese and Sun-Dried Tomatoes

Baked Tomato, Egg and Smoked Mozzarella in Phyllo Cups

Sun-Dried Tomato, Egg and Gorgonzola in Phyllo Strudel

Potato Skins with Egg, Tomato and Brie

Grilled Portobello Mushrooms with Basil Egg Topping

Rolled Cilantro Omelette with Cheddar and Salsa Fresca

Pesto Eggs with Leeks and Asparagus

If you haven't tried leeks, you're in for a real treat—they have a delicious mild onion flavor and are a wonderful enhancement to eggs. Use the white part for this dish and save the green tops for soup stock. Leeks are often grown in sandy soil, so they benefit from a thorough soaking in cold water before use. Change the water a few times until all the sand is removed.

Creamy Pesto Sauce

1 cup dry white wine
3 tablespoons white vinegar
2 tablespoons minced shallots
1½ cups heavy cream
¼ cup fresh Herb Pesto made with basil (recipe follows)

Eggs

4 tablespoons butter
¾ teaspoon minced garlic
¼ cup washed, chopped leeks (white part only)
6 eggs
2 tablespoons half-and-half
4 tablespoons basil pesto (recipe follows)
½ teaspoon pepper
16 blanched asparagus tips
3 tablespoons part skim milk ricotta cheese
2 teaspoons chopped fresh basil
6 slices of Italian or French bread, lightly toasted

SERVES 6

Sauce: In a 2-quart saucepan, reduce the white wine, vinegar and shallots to 2 tablespoons of liquid. Remove the shallots and press out any liquid into the saucepan. Add cream and reduce again by one-third; stir in pesto and keep warm.

Eggs: Preheat oven to 350° F. Melt 2 tablespoons butter in medium skillet. Add garlic and leeks and sauté over medium heat until tender, 1 to 2 minutes. Remove from heat and set aside. Whisk together eggs, half-and-half, pesto and pepper. Melt remaining 2 tablespoons butter in skillet. Pour in egg mixture and cook over medium heat until just beginning to set. Add leeks and asparagus and scramble mixture. Fold in ricotta cheese and remove from heat.

Place the lightly toasted bread slices on a baking sheet; divide egg mixture evenly among them. Heat in oven for 5 minutes and serve with Creamy Pesto Sauce.

Note: The sauce can be made up to 24 hours ahead up to the point that the pesto is added and stored in the refrigerator. Reheat before stirring in the pesto.

HERB PESTO

1 cup fresh herb (basil, tarragon, etc.)
1 tablespoon coarse salt
1 large clove garlic, peeled
2 tablespoons pine nuts
2 tablespoons grated Parmesan (optional)
6 tablespoons extra-virgin olive oil

MAKES 1/2 CUP

TRADITIONALLY, PESTO IS LITERALLY A PASTE, POUNDED, made with a mortar and pestle to grind and combine it. Although efficiently accomplished now with a food processor, there's something wonderfully earthy about grinding pesto by hand—it's the same feeling of kneading fresh bread dough and great for relieving tension. Nine times out of ten (OK, the truth—99 times out of 100), however, I use the food processor for a quick solution.

Combine the basil, salt, garlic and pine nuts in a food processor and process until mixture forms a paste. Add the cheese and process until blended. With the processor still running, add the olive oil in a slow, steady stream. Refrigerate or freeze if not using right away.

NOTES: Other nuts, such as walnuts or almonds, may be used in place of the pine nuts. Different herbs may also be used to create unique dishes.

The basil leaves may be briefly blanched if desired to "fix" their color.

TARRAGON-BAKED EGGS IN BRIOCHE WITH WILD MUSHROOMS AND MADEIRA

THIS BRIOCHE RECIPE MAKES EXTRAS FOR USE IN BREAD pudding or as a delicious snack.

BRIOCHE: Mix the sugar into the warm water until dissolved. Sprinkle the yeast over the warm water to soften and proof, about 5 minutes. In a medium saucepan, heat the milk with the butter until the butter melts. Pour the milk mixture into the bowl of an electric mixer that has a dough hook. Add the sugar and salt and mix until combined. Add the yeast mixture. Add the eggs and mix until smooth. Add 3 cups of flour and mix until smooth.

Switch to the dough hook and add the remaining flour (or incorporate by hand). Mix for about 5 minutes, until the dough pulls away from the sides of the bowl but remains sticky. Cover the bowl with plastic wrap and place in a warm spot to rise until doubled (about 1½ to 2 hours). Punch down the dough and allow to rise again until doubled (about 1 hour).

Brioche

- ½ *teaspoon sugar*
- ¼ *cup warm water*
- 1 *package dry yeast*
- ¼ *cup milk*
- 1 *cup butter*
- ¼ *cup sugar*
- ¾ *teaspoon salt*
- 6 *eggs*
- 5 *cups all-purpose flour*
- 1 *egg yolk*

Eggs and Mushroom Sauté

- 2 *teaspoons chopped fresh tarragon*
- ⅓ *cup heavy cream*
- 4 *tablespoons chopped onion*
- 6 *large eggs*
- 2 *tablespoons butter*
- 1½ *cups chopped shiitake or other mushrooms*
- 3 *tablespoons Madeira*

SERVES 6, WITH EXTRA BRIOCHE

With floured hands, punch down the dough and turn it onto a lightly floured surface. Grease 12 brioche tins. Divide the dough into 13 balls, reserving the extra dough ball for the little "knot" that tops each brioche. Divide the extra ball into 12 tiny balls. Place one large ball in each tin. Make an indentation with your small finger and place a small ball in it. Set the brioches in a warm spot to rise until doubled, about 1½ to 2 hours.

Preheat oven to 375° F. Beat the egg yolk and use a pastry brush to brush the top of each brioche. Bake for 15 minutes or until firm and golden brown.

Sauté: Preheat oven to 375° F. Butter 6 individual ramekins (or one small ovenproof dish). Whisk together the tarragon, heavy cream and chopped onion in a medium bowl. Place 1 egg in each ramekin. Pour the cream mixture over the eggs, dividing it evenly. Bake until set, about 20 minutes.

Melt the butter in a medium sauté pan. Add the chopped mushrooms and sauté over medium heat until soft. Add the Madeira and cook for 2 to 3 minutes longer, until liquid is just absorbed.

Assembly: Slice 6 brioche in half and pinch out their centers. Lightly toast the brioche in the oven for 5 minutes or until slightly dry. Divide the mushrooms among the toasted brioche bottoms. Make slight indentations in the centers and carefully spoon a cooked egg into the center of each. Replace the brioche tops and serve warm.

Notes: Proofing yeast is a small step that will save you wasted hours of wondering why your bread isn't rising if your yeast is no longer active. To proof yeast, add ½ teaspoon of sugar to the warm water, then mix in the yeast. You will know that your yeast cultures still are active if small bubbles appear on the surface of the mixture after a few minutes.

Brioche may be made up to 24 hours in advance and toasted just before serving.

Thin strips of prosciutto added to the mushroom sauté would enhance this dish for those desiring meat.

These are perfect for buffet service since all of the elements are neatly packaged in the brioche. Serve on a bed of fresh watercress for an elegant presentation.

Crab, Egg and Brie Soufflés with Chive Sauce

For those of you on the West Coast, there's been some confusion as to what the best crabs are, so I'm now going to clear it up. Chesapeake Bay blue crabs are without a doubt the best—except of course, if you're from Alaska and fresh king crab is available—but then in Seattle, it's hard to beat a sweet lump of Dungeness. . . . Anyway, whenever your favorite crab is available fresh, treat yourself and a fellow crab lover or two to these delicious soufflés.

Crab Soufflés

- *4 tablespoons butter*
- *2 teaspoons chopped onion*
- *1 cup lump crabmeat*
- *¼ lb. Brie cheese, sliced thinly*
- *¼ cup all-purpose flour*
- *1 teaspoon salt*
- *1¼ cups milk*
- *4 large egg yolks*
- *6 large egg whites, at room temperature*

Chive Sauce

Makes ½ cup

- *1 teaspoon lemon juice*
- *½ cup crème fraîche*
- *3 tablespoons chopped fresh chives*

SERVES 6

Soufflés: Melt 2 tablespoons butter in a medium skillet. Add onion and sauté over medium heat 1 to 2 minutes until translucent. Add crabmeat and heat through. Add Brie, cover pan and remove from heat to soften cheese; set aside.

In a medium saucepan, melt the remaining 2 tablespoons butter. Whisk in the flour and salt and cook for 2 minutes. Heat the milk in a separate pan until just ready to boil. Gradually add half the milk to the flour mixture, whisking until smooth. Stir in the remaining milk and heat mixture to boiling, stirring constantly. Allow to thicken, about 2 minutes, and whisk in the egg yolks. Cook, whisking, for 2 more minutes and remove from heat.

Preheat oven to 375° F. With an electric mixer, beat the whites with a pinch of salt to form stiff peaks; set aside. Fold the crab mixture into the hot milk mixture. Gently fold in half the egg whites to lighten the mixture. Fold in remaining egg whites until just combined.

Butter 6 individual soufflé cups. Make soufflé collars by cutting 6 pieces of waxed paper or aluminum foil about 8 inches long each and fold them in thirds. Butter one side of each collar and wrap it, buttered side in, around the top of the cup. Tie a piece of string around the collar to hold it snugly on the cup. Divide the soufflé mixture among the 6 cups. Bake for 20 to 25 minutes or until puffed and golden brown and the centers are set. Remove the collars and serve immediately, with the chive sauce on the side.

Chive Sauce: Heat lemon juice and crème fraîche until just warm. Stir in chopped chives.

Note: Sauce may be made up to 1 hour ahead and rewarmed over low heat before serving.

Nested Eggs with Potato Blini, Chive Cream and Caviar

Potato Blini

- *3 large red-skinned potatoes, scrubbed but not peeled*
- *2 teaspoons chopped onion*
- *2 tablespoons buttermilk*
- *½ teaspoon white pepper*
- *2 large eggs, separated*
- *¼ cup corn oil*

Chive Cream

- *4 tablespoons cream cheese*
- *4 tablespoons crème fraîche*
- *2 tablespoons chopped fresh chives*

Eggs and Assembly

- *6 large eggs, separated*
- *2 teaspoons black caviar*
- *Cooking spray*

SERVES 6

THE BAD NEWS IS THAT GOOD CAVIAR IS EXPENSIVE; THE good news is that just a fraction of a tiny spoonful is enough to give a wonderful flavor to this elegant dish. Splurge and buy sevruga or beluga caviar for an unforgettable beginning to a special occasion. These blini are little pancakes made with potato in place of the traditional buckwheat flour.

Blini: Finely grate the potatoes into a large bowl. Add the chopped onion, buttermilk and pepper and mix well. Beat the egg yolks lightly and stir into the potato mixture. In a medium bowl or with an electric mixer, whip the egg whites to soft peaks. Fold the egg whites into the potato mixture.

In a large skillet, heat 2 tablespoons of oil over medium heat. For each blini, drop 3 rounded tablespoons of the potato mixture onto the hot oil and flatten with a metal spatula. Cook until crisp and brown around the edges, about 1½ minutes, then flip and cook other side until brown. Drain the blini on a baking sheet lined with paper towels and keep them warm. Add more oil to the pan as necessary to complete 12 cakes.

Cream: Beat cream cheese with an electric mixer until smooth. Add the crème fraîche and beat until smooth and well combined. Stir in the chives and refrigerate until time to serve.

Eggs and Assembly: Preheat oven to 375° F. Whip the egg whites with an electric mixer until stiff but not dry. Lightly grease a baking sheet. Divide the egg whites into 4 small mounds or "nests." Spray lightly with cooking spray. Make an indentation in the center of each nest and spoon an egg yolk into each. Bake for 10 to 12 minutes, until yolk is just set and egg white is lightly browned; avoid overcooking or the yolk will harden. To serve, place 2 warm potato blini on each plate and center an egg nest on top. Spoon on chive cream and top with caviar.

Note: The potato blini may be made up to 24 hours ahead and reheated in a hot oven before serving. The eggs must be baked right before serving.

Egg Strata with Roasted Garlic, Tomatoes and Eggplant

Puff Pastry

- *2 cups all-purpose flour*
- *½ teaspoon salt*
- *1 cup butter*
- *6 tablespoons ice water*
- *1 egg yolk*
- *2 tablespoons milk*

Filling

- *½ cup pitted and finely chopped black olives*
- *½ cup large capers*
- *2 oz. anchovies*
- *1 tablespoon plus 1 teaspoon minced garlic*
- *⅓ cup extra-virgin olive oil*
- *5 cups peeled, diced eggplant*
- *4 eggs, hardcooked and sliced*
- *5 plum tomatoes, thinly sliced*
- *1 teaspoon chopped fresh oregano*
- *2 tablespoons grated Parmesan cheese*

Roasted Garlic

- *5 large garlic heads*
- *2 tablespoons extra-virgin olive oil*

SERVES 6 TO 8

Preceding pages: *Provencal Egg Strata with Roasted Garlic, Tomatoes and Eggplant*

Capers, garlic and anchovies add the Provençal taste to this easy-to-prepare dish. Here is an easier, streamlined version of the classic puff pastry.

Pastry: Combine the flour and salt in a large bowl. Chop the butter into small bits and cut into flour with a pastry blender until crumbly. Add ice water and continue blending until just combined. Gather the dough into a ball and turn it onto a lightly floured surface. With the heel of the hand, push into doughball so that the dough spreads out. Gather dough into a ball again. Roll the dough out into a 14 × 10-inch rectangle. Fold the top quarter down and bottom quarter up so edges of both meet in the center. Fold in half. (This is a "turn.") Wrap and refrigerate the dough for 1 hour. Repeat this process 4 times, allowing the dough to rest 1 hour between turns. Refrigerate the dough at least 2 hours after the final turn, before using. Dough may be frozen at this point for up to 2 weeks or kept in the refrigerator up to 2 days.

Filling: Preheat oven to 375° F. Fit the pastry into a 10- or 11-inch tart pan and trim edges. Line the shell with parchment or foil and fill with pie weights, uncooked beans or rice and bake for 10 minutes. Remove the paper and weights and allow to cool slightly. In a small bowl, stir together the olives, capers, anchovies and 1 teaspoon minced garlic; spread the mixture on the bottom of the pastry.

In a medium skillet, heat the olive oil. Add the remaining minced garlic and sauté over low heat for 30 seconds. Add the eggplant and sauté, stirring occasionally, over medium heat until tender, 10 to 15 minutes. Stir in the roasted garlic cloves. Spread the eggplant mixture in the pastry shell. Arrange the egg slices over the eggplant; arrange the tomato slices, overlapping, over the top. Sprinkle with the oregano and Parmesan. Bake 20 to 25 minutes, until the tart is heated through and the tomatoes are lightly browned on the edges.

Roasted Garlic: Preheat oven to 375° F. Cut ¼ inch off the top of each head. Place in a shallow glass baking dish or clay garlic roaster and drizzle with olive oil. Cover with foil and roast garlic for 1 hour. To use, pick or squeeze out the flesh. Roasted garlic may be stored in the refrigerator for up to 3 days.

Baked Eggs with Pancetta on Shredded Potato Nests

3 large white potatoes, peeled and quartered
1 tablespoon vegetable oil
1 tablespoon butter, melted
½ teaspoon paprika
6 slices of pancetta
6 large eggs
1½ teaspoons chopped fresh basil
1½ teaspoons chopped flat-leaf parsley

SERVES 6

The reason I'm partial to Italian food is not, as you might expect, because I'm part Italian, although I am. I'm also part Irish, and there is no part of me that loves Irish stew. The real reason is that I love to eat, and to me, Italy's cuisine incorporates the most delicious flavors in the world. Every time a "new" cuisine from some part of the world is discovered, I smile and know with confidence that a resurgence of Italian cooking is not far behind. The "foodies" of the world (and I include myself in this group) will always choose what tastes best, regardless of trends. In keeping with this simplistic approach, a delicious ingredient like pancetta—Italian bacon—can take an otherwise ordinary dish and make it extraordinary.

In a medium saucepan, cover the potatoes with cold salted water and bring to a boil. Cook until just tender when pierced with a fork, about 10 minutes; do not cook through. Drain and allow to cool to room temperature.

Preheat oven to 425° F. Coarsely grate the potatoes. Line each of 6 large muffin cups with parchment or waxed paper; combine the oil and butter and generously grease the lined muffin cups. Divide the potatoes among the cups and press them against the bottoms and sides. Bake for about 18 to 20 minutes, until lightly browned. Remove from oven and sprinkle with paprika. Keep potatoes warm.

In a medium skillet, sauté the pancetta over medium-high heat until just brown and drain on paper towels. Chop the pancetta into small bits. Sprinkle the bits equally into the 6 potato nests. Place 1 egg in each nest. Return to the oven and bake 10 to 12 minutes, until the yolk is set and the white is firm. Carefully remove the nests from the cups, peeling off the paper if necessary, sprinkle with basil and parsley and serve warm.

Note: The pancetta may be sautéed 1 to 2 hours in advance. The potatoes may be boiled and grated up to 24 hours in advance and stored, tightly covered, in the refrigerator.

Eggs with Salmon in Dill Crêpes

Dill Crêpes

- ¾ cup all-purpose flour
- 1 egg
- 1 egg yolk
- ½ cup half-and-half
- ½ cup water
- 1 teaspoon lemon zest
- 3 tablespoons finely chopped fresh dill
- 2 tablespoons corn oil or no-stick cooking spray

Smoked Salmon Sauce

- 1 cup dry white wine
- 3 tablespoons white vinegar
- 2 tablespoons minced shallots
- 1½ cups heavy cream
- ½ lb. butter, slightly softened
- ¼ cup chopped smoked salmon

Egg Filling

- 1 cup diced smoked salmon
- 2 tablespoons chopped sweet onion or scallion
- 2 tablespoons finely chopped fresh dill
- 3 tablespoons butter
- 8 large eggs
- ¼ cup half-and-half
- ½ cup crème fraîche
- ½ teaspoon pepper
- ½ teaspoon salt

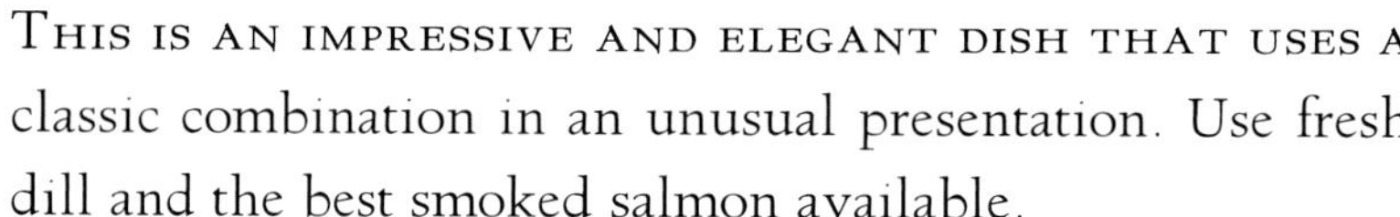

This is an impressive and elegant dish that uses a classic combination in an unusual presentation. Use fresh dill and the best smoked salmon available.

Crêpes: Place the flour in a large mixing bowl and create a well in the center. Whisk together the egg, egg yolk, half-and-half, water, lemon zest and dill. Pour the wet ingredients into the well and whisk to combine.

In a 7- or 8-inch crêpe pan or sauté pan, preheat the oil until hot but not smoking. Pour in ¼ cup batter and swirl quickly to cover pan. Cook over medium heat until crêpe loosens, 1½ to 2 minutes, and flip to cook other side for a few seconds longer. The crêpes should be just lightly browned. Remove the crêpes from pan and cool on a rack; continue until 6 crêpes are completed. Slightly cooled crêpes may be stacked with wax paper in between each.

Sauce: In a 2-quart saucepan, combine the white wine, vinegar and shallots and cook to reduce to 2 tablespoons of liquid. Remove the shallots with a slotted spoon and press out any liquid into the saucepan. Add 1 cup cream and reduce again by one-third. When ready to serve, whisk the softened butter into the warm mixture over low heat. In a food processor or blender, process the smoked salmon and the remaining ½ cup of heavy cream until well blended. Whisk the smoked salmon mixture into the sauce on low heat. Keep sauce warm until ready to serve.

Filling: In a small mixing bowl, toss the smoked salmon, onion and dill together. Melt the butter in a large skillet. Add the smoked salmon mixture and sauté lightly over medium heat until just cooked. Whisk together the eggs, half-and-half, crème fraîche and salt and pepper. Pour into the skillet over the salmon mixture and scramble until just cooked. Assemble crêpes immediately.

ASSEMBLY

½ cup crème fraîche

2 tablespoons chopped fresh chives

SERVES 6

ASSEMBLY: Preheat oven to 350° F. Divide the egg mixture evenly among the centers of each crêpe. Spoon 1 tablespoon of crème fraîche over each of the fillings and roll crêpes. Place the crêpes, seam side down, on a baking sheet and heat for 5 minutes. To serve, place 1 crêpe on each plate and spoon the sauce over. Sprinkle with chopped chives and serve.

NOTES: The crêpes may be made ahead of time (layered in waxed paper and stored in an airtight container) for easy assembly.

The smoked salmon sauce would also be delicious on corn waffles or pancakes.

For buffet service, gather the crêpes into little bundles or "beggar's purses" tied up with a blanched strip of scallion or chive.

The sauce may be prepared through the cream reduction, cooled to room temperature, and held in the refrigerator until 1 hour before serving. Reheat carefully over low heat.

Truffled Risotto Eggs with Spinach and Shaved Parmesan

6 cups fresh cleaned spinach
3 tablespoons extra-virgin olive oil
½ cup chopped onions
2 cups arborio rice
6 cups chicken stock
1 tablespoon grated black truffles
6 large eggs
2 tablespoons butter
3 tablespoons pine nuts
3 to 4 oz. large shavings of Parmesan

SERVES 6

We visited the Italian region of Umbria in winter 1995 and discovered the allure of black magic—the tuber known as the black truffle. During the height of the season, fresh truffles are grated or sliced onto everything from luxurious meat dishes to basic scrambled eggs. One of my favorite truffle dishes is *risotto con tartuffi,* quite simply "rice with truffles." This dish was inspired by such divine simplicity.

Bring 1 quart of lightly salted cold water to a boil in a medium saucepan. Submerge the spinach in the boiling water all at once, then immediately drain and refresh in a bowl of ice water. Squeeze dry and finely chop. Set aside.

In a large skillet, heat the oil. Add the onions and sauté over medium heat until translucent, 2 to 3 minutes. Add the rice and stir to coat with oil. In the meantime, in a separate saucepan, bring the chicken stock to a boil, them remove it from the heat. Add 1 cup of the hot stock to the rice and simmer over medium heat, stirring constantly until the liquid is almost all absorbed. Continue adding hot stock, ½ cup at a time, stirring constantly until the rice is creamy and just tender, about 25 minutes. Stir in the truffles.

In a small bowl, whisk together the eggs. Pour the eggs all at once into the rice and stir rapidly to scramble and combine while cooking; remove from heat. Melt the butter in a medium sauté pan. Add the pine nuts and cook over medium heat for 1 minute. Add the spinach and heat through, about 2 minutes. Divide the spinach among 6 plates, creating a well in the center. Spoon the truffled risotto and egg mixture into the center. Sprinkle the Parmesan shavings on top and serve warm.

Note: The risotto must be stirred constantly to achieve the proper consistency. Resist the temptation to add more than ½ cup stock at a time, since the rice requires slow absorption to cook properly. Toward the end, taste a grain of the rice at 1- to 2-minute intervals to ensure that the rice is tender and cooked through.

Eggs "Oscar" with Lobster, Asparagus Tips and Tarragon Rounds

THIS DISH WAS CREATED DURING OUR SUMMERS IN Maine, delighting our guests, who could truly have lobster for breakfast, lunch, and dinner. It was inspired by two wonderful but perhaps heavy-handed dishes—Veal Oscar, a cutlet topped with asparagus and bearnaise sauce, and Eggs Benedict, poached eggs with Canadian bacon on English muffins topped with hollandaise sauce. In this dish, the tarragon flavor that distinguishes bearnaise is added to the muffin base, eliminating the need for the ultra-rich sauce. The dish is presented like Eggs Benedict, but instead the tarragon rounds are topped with flavorful sautéed lobster and poached eggs, and served with tender asparagus tips.

Tarragon Rounds

- *2 cups all-purpose flour*
- *3 tablespoons cornmeal*
- *2 teaspoons baking powder*
- *½ teaspoon salt*
- *½ teaspoon baking soda*
- *½ cup butter*
- *¾ cup buttermilk*
- *2 tablespoons chopped fresh tarragon*
- *2 tablespoons milk*

Eggs

- *2 tablespoons butter*
- *1 tablespoon chopped shallots*
- *1 lb. cooked Maine lobster meat*
- *2 tablespoons heavy cream*
- *6 large eggs (for poaching)*

Assembly

- *1 tablespoon butter*
- *24 spears fresh asparagus, peeled from the tips down and blanched*
- *6 tarragon rounds*
- *2 teaspoons chopped flat-leaf parsley*

SERVES 6

ROUNDS: Preheat oven to 450° F. In a large mixing bowl, combine the flour, cornmeal, baking powder, salt and baking soda. With a pastry blender, cut in the butter until crumbly. Stir in the buttermilk until just combined. Stir in the tarragon. Lightly grease a baking sheet. Drop 2 tablespoons of batter onto sheet for each of 6 rounds. Spread the batter into circles 3 inches in diameter. Smooth the tops with the back of a spoon dipped in milk. Bake for 12 to 15 minutes, until lightly browned. Remove from oven and keep warm.

EGGS: Melt the butter in a small saucepan. Sauté the shallots over low heat for 1 minute. Add the lobster meat and cook until just heated through. Add the cream, cook for 1 minute and remove from heat; set aside.

Poach the eggs either in poaching cups, or by the following method: Bring 6 cups water plus ½ cup wine vinegar to a boil in a deep saucepan. Turn down the heat and break the eggs open, easing them into the water one at a time. Keeping eggs separated, cook 3 to 5 minutes, depending on desired degree of doneness, and remove with a slotted spoon; rinse the eggs briefly with fresh water.

ASSEMBLY: Melt the remaining 1 tablespoon butter in a medium sauté pan. Sauté the asparagus until just warmed through. Place 4 asparagus spears on each of 6 individual plates. Place a tarragon round on each plate, alongside the asparagus. Top each round with sautéed lobster meat and a poached egg. Sprinkle with parsley and serve.

Cilantro Corn Pudding with Scallions, Peppers and Monterey Jack Cheese

1 tablespoon butter
½ cup chopped scallions
1 cup milk
2 cups fresh corn kernels
2 tablespoons cornstarch
3 eggs
½ cup chicken stock
½ teaspoon black pepper
⅛ teaspoon cayenne pepper
4 roasted chile peppers, skinned, seeded and finely chopped
1 cup Monterey Jack cheese, diced
½ cup chopped fresh cilantro

SERVES 6 TO 8

Cilantro is an inspiration in itself. Its fresh, unusual flavor enhances cuisines ranging from Mexican to Thai. This is a southwest-inspired "pudding" that slices like corn bread.

Preheat oven to 375° F. Grease an 8-inch-square baking pan. In a small sauté pan, melt the butter. Add the scallions and cook over low heat about 4 minutes, until softened; remove from heat and set aside to cool.

In a food processor, whiz together the milk, corn kernels and cornstarch until combined. In a large bowl, whisk the eggs. Whisk the corn–milk mixture into the eggs until combined. Whisk in the chicken stock and black and cayenne peppers. Stir in the sautéed scallions, chile peppers and cheese, then the cilantro. Spoon the batter into the prepared baking pan. Place the pan in a larger deep pan and fill the outer pan with hot water to reach about halfway up the smaller pan. Bake for 50 to 60 minutes, until the pudding is lightly browned and the center is set. Cut into squares and serve warm.

Notes: The corn pudding may be baked up to 24 hours ahead and reheated in a 350° F oven for 7 minutes before serving.

Crème fraîche and fresh salsa would be delicious accompaniments.

Baked Eggs with Basil Pancakes and Plum Tomato Confit

Pancakes

- *¼ cup butter, melted*
- *⅔ cup buttermilk*
- *1 egg*
- *1 cup all-purpose flour*
- *1 cup cornmeal*
- *1 tablespoon sugar*
- *1 teaspoon baking soda*
- *½ teaspoon salt*
- *½ cup water*
- *2 tablespoons chopped fresh basil*
- *¼ cup corn oil*

Baked Eggs and Tomato Confit

- *6 eggs*
- *3 tablespoons heavy cream*
- *1 tablespoon extra-virgin olive oil*
- *2 tablespoons chopped shallots*
- *1 cup seeded and chopped plum tomatoes*
- *2 teaspoons chopped fresh basil*

SERVES 6

These little pancakes are a "kick"—a unique little treat to enliven eggs. Fresh basil and sweet plum tomato have summer written all over their taste.

Pancakes: In a small bowl, whisk together the butter, buttermilk and egg. In a larger bowl, mix together the flour, cornmeal, sugar, baking soda, and salt. Stir in the butter mixture until just combined. Stir in the water and basil. In a large skillet, heat a few tablespoons of oil over medium heat. Drop the batter by tablespoonfuls into the hot oil, making 18 1½- to 2-inch cakes. Cook until bubbles start to form on the top and the edges are slightly browned, 1 to 2 minutes, then carefully flip and cook on the other side for about 1 minute. Remove the pancakes from the pan and drain them on paper towels.

Eggs and Confit: Preheat oven to 350° F. Lightly butter or grease 6 individual ramekins or custard cups. Break 1 egg in each cup; top each with ½ tablespoon cream. Place the egg cups in a rectangular baking pan and fill the pan with hot water until two-thirds full. Bake the eggs for 6 minutes or until they reach the desired degree of doneness.

In the meantime, heat the oil in a medium sauté pan. Add the shallots and sauté over high heat for 30 seconds. Add the tomatoes, sauté for 10 seconds and immediately remove from heat; stir in the basil.

Assembly: Arrange 3 warm pancakes on each of 6 individual plates. With a tablespoon, scoop the eggs from the cups onto the pancakes. Spoon tomato confit over and serve.

Notes: The pancakes may be made up to 24 hours ahead, reheated and "recrisped" in a hot oven at 375° F for 5 minutes.

The pancakes are also wonderful when made with fresh chives, white corn and scallions.

Rolled Basil Soufflé with Roasted Red Pepper Coulis

Combining the elegance of a soufflé with the ease of an omelette, this jelly-roll–style egg dish will impress your guests.

Rolled Basil Soufflé

- *¼ cup butter*
- *½ cup all-purpose flour*
- *½ teaspoon salt*
- *½ teaspoon pepper*
- *2½ cups milk, scalded*
- *5 eggs, separated*
- *2 tablespoons basil pesto*

Filling

- *1 tablespoon extra-virgin olive oil*
- *1 tablespoon minced shallots*
- *¼ cup chopped prosciutto*
- *1½ cups chopped shiitake mushrooms*
- *5 oz. crumbled goat cheese*
- *5 oz. cream cheese*
- *½ cup chopped roasted red peppers*

Coulis and Assembly

- *½ cup chopped roasted red peppers*
- *¼ cup fresh tomato sauce*
- *2 tablespoons chopped fresh basil*

Serves 6

Soufflé: Preheat oven to 350° F. Grease a 15½ × 10½ × 1-inch jelly-roll pan, line with parchment or waxed paper; grease the parchment or paper. Melt the butter in a saucepan. Stir in the flour, salt and pepper and cook over low heat, stirring, for 2 minutes. Add the warm milk and bring to a boil. Lower heat and simmer for 2 minutes. Whisk in the egg yolks and cook 1 minute longer. Remove from heat and allow to cool, stirring occasionally. Beat the egg whites until stiff. Stir the pesto into the cooled mixture, then carefully fold in the whipped egg whites. Spread the mixture into the prepared pan and bake for 15 to 20 minutes, until firm and just lightly browned. Immediately invert the roll onto a dish towel topped with parchment or waxed paper and roll up jelly-roll style. Allow to cool.

Filling: Heat the olive oil in a medium sauté pan. Add the shallots and sauté over medium heat for 30 seconds. Add the prosciutto and mushrooms and sauté for 2 to 3 minutes, until mushrooms soften. Remove from heat and cool slightly. Stir in the goat cheese, cream cheese and peppers and allow to soften to spreading consistency.

Unroll the soufflé and spread on the filling. Roll up the soufflé without the towel or paper, place on a lightly greased baking sheet and cover with foil. Bake for 10 minutes at 350° F.

Coulis: Process the roasted peppers and tomato sauce in a food processor or blender until smooth.

Assembly: To serve, heat the puréed sauce in a small saucepan and spoon equal pools of warm sauce onto 6 plates. Remove the roll from the oven and slice it into 12 even pieces. Place 2 slices on each plate and sprinkle with chopped basil. Serve immediately.

Notes: The coulis may be made a day ahead and stored in the refrigerator. Roasted peppers will keep up to 1 week in the refrigerator. The roll may be made ahead and refrigerated before the final baking.

Try different fillings, cheeses and herbs such as smoked salmon and dill or chopped scallions; Cheddar and cilantro; crab and Camembert.

Basil Crêpes with Ricotta, Eggs, Onions and Artichokes

Basil Crêpes

- *¾ cup all-purpose flour*
- *1 egg*
- *1 egg yolk*
- *½ cup half-and-half*
- *½ cup water*
- *3 tablespoons chopped fresh basil*
- *2 tablespoons corn oil or no-stick cooking spray*

Eggs

- *6 eggs*
- *1 tablespoon half-and-half*
- *1 tablespoon butter*
- *¼ cup sliced sweet onions*
- *¾ cup quartered cooked baby artichoke hearts*
- *1¼ cups ricotta cheese*
- *Basil leaves*

SERVES 6

It's hard to keep a good dish down (or something like that), so here's another version of crêpes, this time flavored with basil and filled with tender artichokes.

Crêpes: Place the flour in a large mixing bowl and create a well in the center. Whisk together the egg, egg yolk, half-and-half and water. Pour the wet ingredients into the well and whisk to combine. Stir in the basil. In a 7- or 8-inch crêpe pan or sauté pan, preheat the oil until hot but not smoking or use no-stick spray. For each crêpe, pour ¼ cup batter into the pan and swirl quickly to cover the bottom. Cook over medium heat until crêpe is loose, 1½ to 2 minutes, then flip to cook the other side briefly. The crêpes should be lightly browned. Remove the crêpes from pan as they cook and cool on a rack. Continue until 6 crêpes have been completed.

Eggs: In a medium bowl, whisk together the eggs and half-and-half. Melt the butter in a medium skillet. Add the onions and sauté over medium heat until just soft and translucent, about 2 minutes. Add the artichoke hearts and sauté until just warmed through. Stir in the eggs all at once and scramble until just done. Remove from heat and stir in 1 cup of the ricotta cheese until just combined.

Assembly: To serve, preheat oven to 375° F. Divide egg mixture among the crêpes, then roll each crêpe up and place seam side down on a lightly greased baking sheet. Bake for 10 minutes. Remove from oven and garnish each crêpe with a tablespoon of ricotta and basil leaves.

Note: Slightly cooled crêpes may be stacked with waxed paper and stored in an airtight container for up to 24 hours in advance.

Asparagus, Chèvre and Roasted Pepper Napoleon with Pepper Cream

1 sheet puff pastry (page 72)
6 eggs
3 tablespoons half-and-half
2 tablespoons butter
6 pastry rectangles
12 asparagus spears, blanched
4 oz. goat cheese
4 roasted red peppers, seeded and peeled
3 tablespoons red wine
1 shallot, peeled and chopped
1 cup heavy cream
1 teaspoon white pepper

SERVES 6

PUFF PASTRY CAN BE MADE UP TO 2 WEEKS AHEAD and frozen until ready to use.

To make the napoleon shells, preheat oven to 375° F. Roll out the pastry f inch thick and cut into 6 2 5 6-inch rectangles. Place the rectangles on a lightly greased baking sheet. Whisk together the egg yolk and milk and brush the top of each shell with the mixture. Bake for 15 minutes or until pastry puffs and is lightly browned. Set aside.

In a large mixing bowl, whisk together the eggs and half-and-half. On low heat, melt the butter in a large sauté pan. Add the eggs and allow them to set just until cooked through, like a very thin omelette. Remove from heat.

Preheat oven to 375° F. Cut each piece of pastry in half. Cut 3 of the peppers into halves. Cut the egg mixture into 6 rectangles. Layer egg, asparagus, goat cheese and roasted pepper onto 6 pieces of pastry. Top each with a second rectangle of pastry and bake for 7 to 10 minutes, until heated through.

In the meantime, place the red wine and shallot in a medium saucepan. Reduce by half over medium heat. Remove and discard the shallot and add the heavy cream to the pan. Continue cooking over medium heat until reduced by one-third. Pour half the reduced cream into a food processor or blender and add the remaining red pepper. Whiz until smooth, then whisk back into remaining cream; whisk in white pepper. Serve each napoleon on a pool of red pepper cream.

NOTES: The egg can be omitted and the napoleons incorporated into a more elaborate menu, such as part of a brunch buffet.

Phyllo leaves can be substituted for the puff pastry, which will make crisper layers and a lower-fat dish.

Save scraps of puff pastry and use tiny cookie cutters to make tasty, decorative croutons for soup.

Store-bought puff pastry is a labor-saving substitute, but if you have the time, try making the pastry from scratch. It's easy and delicious.

Smoked Trout Frittata

4 red potatoes, halved
½ teaspoon salt
3 eggs
3 egg whites
¼ cup milk
½ teaspoon white pepper
2 teaspoons extra-virgin olive oil
1 cup sliced sweet onion
1 cup flaked smoked trout
1 tablespoon chopped fresh dill
1 tablespoon freshly grated horseradish

SERVES 6

Many egg dishes may be lowered in fat by replacing some of the whole eggs with egg whites and using milk in lieu of cream or half-and-half. This hearty dish, with its wonderful mix of tastes and textures, is a good example of lowering fat without compromising taste.

In a medium saucepan, cover the potatoes with cold water, add the salt and bring to a boil. Cook for 15 to 20 minutes or until just tender. Drain and cool. Cut the potatoes into thin slices. In a medium bowl, whisk together eggs, egg whites, milk and pepper. Heat olive oil in a medium skillet. Add the onions and sauté over low heat for 2 to 3 minutes, until soft and translucent. Remove the pan from the heat and arrange the potatoes over the onions. Distribute the trout over the potatoes and gently pour the eggs over all. Cover the pan and return it to low heat. Cook until eggs are set, about 6 to 8 minutes.

Meanwhile, preheat the broiler. Place the skillet under the broiler until the eggs are cooked and just beginning to brown. Remove the pan, and sprinkle with the dill and horseradish. Cut the frittata into wedges and serve.

Wild Rice and Scallion Egg Tarts in Herb Crust

Tart Shell

- *1½ cups all-purpose flour*
- *2 teaspoons chopped fresh tarragon*
- *1 tablespoon chopped flat-leaf parsley*
- *½ teaspoon salt*
- *½ cup cold butter, cut into bits*
- *3 tablespoons solid vegetable shortening*
- *4 tablespoons ice water*

Filling

- *4 eggs*
- *3 tablespoons half-and-half*
- *1 teaspoon chopped flat-leaf parsley*
- *2 tablespoons extra-virgin olive oil*
- *2 cups cooked wild rice*
- *1 cup chopped scallions*

SERVES 6

Wild rice is not really rice at all; it's actually the seed of a wild grass. My husband once foraged with a friend for wild rice during his teaching tenure in Minnesota. Basically, the two men paddled their canoe out into the wild-rice flats, shook the grass briskly until the canoe was completely filled with rice, then paddled back to shore. The entire operation took about 5 minutes. Here, the nutty taste of wild rice combines with scallion and eggs for a delicious morning meal.

Crust: With a food processor or pastry blender, combine the flour, tarragon, parsley, salt, butter and shortening until just crumbly. Add the ice water, 1 tablespoon at a time, until dough begins to form a ball. Allow the dough to rest at room temperature 10 minutes.

Preheat oven to 375° F. Roll out dough on a lightly floured surface to fit into a 10- or 11-inch tart pan. Place dough in pan and prick with a fork. Line with parchment or foil and add pie weights, uncooked rice or beans to weigh down the shell. Bake for 8 minutes, remove liner, and bake 8 minutes more or until lightly browned. Remove from oven and cool.

Filling: Whisk together eggs, half-and-half and parsley. Heat the olive oil in a medium skillet. Add the wild rice and scallions and sauté, stirring, for 2 minutes. Remove from heat and cool slightly. Spread the rice mixture in the pastry shell. Pour the egg mixture over top and bake for 20 to 25 minutes or until set.

Note: Individual tarts can be made in 6 small pans with removable bottoms.

Asparagus Egg Tart with Roquefort, White Wine and Cracked Pepper

Tart Shell

- *1½ cups all-purpose flour*
- *3 tablespoons coarsely ground pepper*
- *½ teaspoon salt*
- *½ cup cold butter, cut into bits*
- *3 tablespoons solid vegetable shortening*
- *4 tablespoons ice water*

Filling

- *3 eggs*
- *¼ cup half-and-half*
- *3 tablespoons chopped flat-leaf parsley*
- *¼ teaspoon cayenne pepper*
- *1 tablespoon butter*
- *1 cup chopped blanched asparagus (about 10 to 12 stalks)*
- *1 tablespoon flour*
- *½ cup white wine*
- *1 teaspoon lemon juice*
- *1 cup crumbled Roquefort cheese*
- *12 blanched asparagus tips*

SERVES 6 TO 8

Fine imported Roquefort from France has no rival; its robust flavor is a natural pairing for tender asparagus. This egg tart is easily prepared ahead and either kept warm or reheated for serving.

Shell: With a food processor or pastry blender, combine the flour, pepper, salt, butter and shortening until just crumbly. Add the ice water, 1 tablespoon at a time, until dough begins to form a ball. Allow the dough to rest at room temperature 10 minutes.

Preheat oven to 375° F. Roll out dough on a lightly floured surface to fit into an 11-inch tart pan. Place dough in shell and prick with a fork. Line with parchment or foil and add pie weights, uncooked rice or beans to weigh down the shell. Bake for 8 minutes, remove liner, and bake 8 minutes more or until lightly browned. Remove from oven and set aside to cool.

Filling: Whisk together the eggs and half-and-half. Stir in the parsley and cayenne pepper; set aside. In a medium skillet, melt the butter over medium heat. Add the chopped asparagus and sauté for 1 minute. Sprinkle on the flour and sauté, stirring, 1 minute more. Add the white wine and lemon juice and cook until slightly thickened, about 1 to 2 minutes. Remove from heat. Stir in the Roquefort.

Assembly: Spread the asparagus-Roquefort mixture in the bottom of the prebaked shell and pour the egg mixture over. Arrange the asparagus tips in the center of the tart. Bake for 25 minutes at 375° F or until set and golden brown.

Note: Individual tarts can be made in 6 small pans with removable bottoms.

CRISP NOODLE CAKES WITH SHRIMP, CHINESE BLACK BEANS AND POACHED EGGS

NOODLE CAKES

½ cup corn oil

2 cups cooked angel hair pasta, refreshed in cold water and drained

SHRIMP WITH LEMON GRASS

1 cup fish stock

1 tablespoon fish sauce

¾ lb. large shrimp, shelled and deveined

3 stalks fresh lemon grass, sliced into 1-inch lengths

¼ cup chopped scallions

3 tablespoons fresh lime juice

1 cup bean sprouts

EGGS AND BLACK BEANS

6 eggs

1 tablespoon corn oil

1 teaspoon sesame oil

1 teaspoon minced garlic

¼ cup Chinese black beans

ASSEMBLY

2 teaspoons chopped flat-leaf parsley

SERVES 6

CHINESE FERMENTED BLACK BEANS ARE HEAVILY SALTED and can benefit from a good soaking to remove some of the brine. Here, enhanced by lemon grass, they add a unique Asian flavor to breakfast.

NOODLE CAKES: Heat the oil in a large skillet over medium-high heat to approximately 375° F. Drop ⅓ cup pasta into the hot oil at a time. Using tongs or a long fork, form 6 little "nests." Cook each nest for 1 to 2 minutes, or until just beginning to brown; turn over and cook for 30 seconds more. Remove from oil and drain on paper towels; keep warm.

SHRIMP: Combine the stock, fish sauce and lemon grass in a medium sauté pan and bring to a boil. Add the shrimp and poach until just pink and cooked through, about 4 minutes. Stir in the chopped scallions, lime juice and bean sprouts and cook for 1 minute more. Remove from heat and keep warm.

EGGS: Poach the eggs to desired degree of doneness (see page 77). Heat the corn oil and sesame oil in a small skillet. Add the garlic and black beans and sauté over medium heat until just heated through, about 1 minute. Remove from heat.

ASSEMBLY: Drain off any excess liquid from the shrimp. Divide the shrimp and bean sprout mixture among 6 plates. Set a nest on each plate and top with a poached egg. Top each egg with black beans, sprinkle with parsley and serve.

NOTES: The nests may be made up to 24 hours in advance and reheated in a 375° F oven for 4 to 5 minutes, but be careful they do not overbrown.

To remove brine from black beans, soak in 2 cups cold water for 1 hour.

OPPOSITE: *Crisp Noodle Cakes with Shrimp, Chinese Black Beans and Poached Eggs; Spring Rolls with Wild Mushrooms, Goat Cheese and Sun-Dried Tomatoes*

Spring Rolls with Wild Mushrooms, Goat Cheese and Sun-Dried Tomatoes

THE PERFECT BUFFET ITEM OR BREAKFAST TREAT FOR people on the go, these spring rolls may be baked or fried according to preference. The sun-dried tomato and goat cheese dipping sauce is sublime and may be made up to a day in advance.

Sauce

- *¼ cup chopped sun-dried tomatoes*
- *1 cup white wine*
- *2 tablespoons chopped shallots*
- *2 cups heavy cream*
- *½ cup goat cheese, crumbled*

Spring Rolls

- *1 16-oz. package (about 2 cups) Asian cellophane noodles (available at Asian groceries or specialty shops)*
- *2 tablespoons butter*
- *1 cup chopped shiitake mushrooms*
- *¼ cup chopped scallions*
- *3 eggs*
- *6 spring roll wrappers*
- *Oil for frying*

SERVES 6

SAUCE: Soak the sun-dried tomatoes in a bowl of hot water to soften for 15 to 20 minutes. In a medium saucepan, simmer the white wine and shallots until the liquid is reduced to about 2 tablespoons. Remove the shallots and pour in the heavy cream. Bring to a gentle boil, then lower the heat and simmer until reduced by one-half. Remove from heat and stir in the crumbled goat cheese. Drain the sun-dried tomatoes and stir them into the sauce. Keep warm or refrigerate if not using right away.

SPRING ROLLS: Soak the noodles in a bowl of hot water until softened, about 20 minutes. Rinse noodles, drain and set aside. Melt the butter in a large sauté pan. Add the chopped mushrooms and sauté over medium heat until just softened. Stir in the scallions and cook for 30 seconds. Whisk the eggs together and stir into the mushroom mixture; cook until just done. Remove the pan from heat and stir in the cellophane noodles until well combined.

Lay out a spring roll wrapper with a point facing toward you and put about ½ cup of filling in the low center. Fold the bottom point up over the filling, fold in the two side points, then continue rolling until a tight, neat package is formed. Repeat with the remaining wrappers. Heat the oil to 360° F. Fry 3 rolls at a time until browned and crisp on all sides. Drain on paper towels and serve with the warm sauce.

NOTES: Smaller buffet- or cocktail-size egg rolls can be made by cutting each spring roll wrapper into 4 pieces and dividing the filling accordingly.

The rolls can be baked, rather than fried, in a preheated 375° F oven for 12 to 15 minutes. Spray on a little no-stick cooking spray for the last 5 minutes to achieve a crisper spring roll.

Baked Tomato, Egg and Smoked Mozzarella in Phyllo Cups

4 tablespoons butter
5 sheets of phyllo dough
2 tablespoons chopped shallots
6 eggs
2 tablespoons half-and-half
3 plum tomatoes, sliced
½ cup shredded smoked mozzarella
2 teaspoons chopped chives

SERVES 6

CRISP PHYLLO IS LAYERED INTO FLOWERLIKE CUPS FOR this elegant presentation. Fresh plum tomatoes and smoked Italian mozzarella cheese are a natural, traditional pairing in the easily assembled filling.

Preheat oven to 375° F. Melt 2 tablespoons of butter. With a sharp knife, cut the phyllo sheets into quarters. Lightly grease or butter a muffin pan for 6 large muffins. Take one quarter-sheet of phyllo dough and brush it lightly with the melted butter. Layer on a second sheet, slightly askew (so the corners do not meet) and brush with butter. Layer on a third sheet, also askew. Fit the layered pastry into the bottom of one of the muffin cups and press into the bottom to flatten, with pointed ends standing straight up. Repeat with the remaining dough to form 6 cups. Brush with any remaining butter and bake for 8 to 10 minutes until lightly browned. Cool the shells slightly in the pan, then carefully remove them to a baking sheet.

Melt the remaining 2 tablespoons of butter in a medium sauté pan. Add the shallots and sauté over medium-low heat for 1 minute. Whisk together the eggs and half-and-half. Pour into sauté pan and cook, stirring occasionally, until cooked through but still glossy. Remove from heat. Spoon egg mixture into each cup. Place two tomato slices on each cup, then sprinkle with smoked mozzarella. Bake for 5 minutes or until cheese is just melted. Sprinkle with chives and serve immediately.

NOTE: The phyllo cups may be baked a day ahead and stored in an airtight container. They may also be made in mini-muffin pans for an hors d'oeuvre–sized buffet item.

Sun-Dried Tomato, Egg and Gorgonzola in Phyllo Strudel

¼ cup sun-dried tomatoes, softened in hot water
2 tablespoons butter
2 tablespoons chopped shallots
6 large eggs
3 tablespoons half-and-half
3 tablespoons extra-virgin olive oil
3 sheets phyllo pastry
½ cup crumbled gorgonzola cheese
2 oz. anchovies, chopped
¼ cup small capers
¼ cup pitted black olives, coarsely chopped
1 teaspoon minced garlic

SERVES 6

Savory strudels, like their sweet counterparts, are made easily with store-bought phyllo dough. Almost any combination could be used as a filling, but this meatless version is enlivened with the tang of blue cheese. A quickly assembled tapenade adds color and pizzazz to the final presentation.

Drain the sun-dried tomatoes and chop into small pieces. In a medium sauté pan, melt the butter. Add the shallots and cook over low heat for 2 minutes. Whisk together the eggs and half-and-half and pour into the sauté pan. Scramble over medium-low heat until just done but still soft and glossy; remove from heat and cool slightly.

Preheat oven to 375° F. Lightly grease a baking sheet. Remove and set aside 1 tablespoon olive oil. Lay out 1 full sheet of phyllo and brush with olive oil. Top with a second sheet, brush with oil and top with the third sheet. Spread the egg filling along one of the longer edges. Sprinkle on the sun-dried tomatoes and gorgonzola cheese and roll up jelly-roll style. Brush the roll with olive oil and bake for 15 to 20 minutes, until lightly browned and crisp.

In a small bowl, combine the reserved 1 tablespoon olive oil with the anchovies, capers, olives and garlic. Divide the olive mixture among 6 plates and top with slices of the warm strudel.

Notes: Strudels may be made individually for ease of serving. To make individual strudels, use 6 sheets of phyllo instead of three. Lay out 1 full sheet, brush with olive oil and fold in half lengthwise. Spread ⅙ of the egg filling on the lower short edge, sprinkle on ⅙ of the sun-dried tomatoes and gorgonzola and roll up jelly-roll style. Repeat until 6 individual strudels are formed.

For a decorative effect, use blanched chives to tie the ends of each strudel before baking if desired. Brush the rolls with olive oil and continue with the recipe.

Potato Skins with Egg, Tomato and Brie

3 large baking potatoes
1 tablespoon butter
6 eggs
2 tablespoons half-and-half
3 plum tomatoes, sliced
6 oz. Brie cheese, thinly sliced
2 tablespoons chopped flat-leaf parsley

SERVES 6

In the market where I pick out my winter produce, there's a wonderful kosher deli with an array of salads and "pop-in-the-oven" meals. Their ready-made potatoes inspired me to create this breakfast version of potato skins.

Preheat oven to 375° F. Prick potatoes all over with a fork. Place potatoes on a baking sheet and bake for 1 to 1½ hours, until cooked through; allow to cool. Slice cooled potatoes in half and remove the flesh; reserve flesh for another use. Place the shells on a baking sheet. Melt the butter in a medium sauté pan. Whisk together the eggs and half-and-half and pour into pan. Scramble rapidly until just cooked but glossy. Fill each potato shell with egg, and top with sliced tomatoes and Brie. Bake on the bottom rack of the preheated oven for 12 minutes. Sprinkle with parsley and serve.

NOTES: The potatoes can be baked up to 24 hours in advance.

Try different variations such as spinach and Cheddar or prosciutto and gorgonzola for a breakfast or brunch buffet.

Grilled Portobello Mushrooms with Basil Egg Topping

6 large Portobello mushrooms

2 large garlic cloves, finely chopped

½ cup extra-virgin olive oil

6 large eggs

2 tablespoons half-and-half

1 tablespoon butter

½ cup ricotta cheese

½ cup chopped fresh basil leaves

½ cup chopped fresh flat-leaf parsley

2 tablespoons balsamic vinegar

3 large plum tomatoes, seeded and coarsely chopped

SERVES 6

Portobello mushrooms have a meaty texture that holds up wonderfully to grilling. They also make a perfect substitute in egg dishes that require a muffin or bread base and turn an ordinary dish into a special treat.

Remove stems from mushrooms. In a blender or food processor, combine the garlic and olive oil and blend. Brush both sides of each mushroom with garlic oil. Preheat the broiler; broil each mushroom about 3 minutes on each side, until just cooked. Remove from broiler and keep warm.

Whisk together the eggs and half-and-half. Melt the butter in a medium sauté pan. Add the eggs and stir over medium heat until they are soft and glossy; stir in the ricotta cheese and continue cooking for 2 to 3 minutes. Remove from heat and stir in basil and parsley. Place mushrooms, undersides up, on individual plates. Sprinkle with balsamic vinegar and spoon on the egg mixture. Top with chopped tomato and serve.

NOTES: Flat-leaf parsley, also known as Italian parsley, has a milder flavor than the curly variety. This is a delicious herb that's easily grown in a window box or clay pot. If flat-leaf parsley is unavailable substitute ¼ cup chopped curly parsley.

Use only the finest imported balsamic vinegar (I like the Fini brand, available at specialty stores and through Williams Sonoma mail order)—it's expensive, but a little goes a long way.

Rolled Cilantro Omelette with Cheddar and Salsa Fresca

Salsa Fresca

- *1 teaspoon minced jalapeño pepper*
- *2 cups seeded and chopped plum tomatoes*
- *¼ cup chopped onion*
- *3 tablespoons chopped scallions*
- *2 tablespoons chopped fresh cilantro*

Omelette

- *1 cup milk*
- *6 eggs*
- *½ cup all-purpose flour*
- *¼ cup butter, melted*
- *¼ teaspoon cayenne pepper*
- *2 teaspoons chopped fresh cilantro*
- *1 seeded and finely chopped jalapeño pepper*
- *1 cup shredded Cheddar cheese*
- *1 cup seeded and chopped tomato*

SERVES 6 TO 8

Cilantro, also known as coriander or Chinese parsley, is an annual herb easily grown from seed. When the cilantro plant goes to seed, it produces delicate white flowers, which make a perfect garnish, and tiny coriander seeds, which are used often in curries.

Salsa: Mix ingredients together in a medium bowl and refrigerate until ready to use.

Omelette: Preheat oven to 400° F. Grease a 15½ x 100½-inch jelly-roll pan, line with parchment and grease again. Combine the milk, eggs, flour, butter, cayenne pepper, chopped cilantro and jalapeño pepper in the bowl of an electric mixer. Mix on medium speed until frothy and well blended. Pour into the pan and bake 18 to 20 minutes or until roll is set and slightly puffed. Remove from oven and sprinkle with the Cheddar cheese and chopped tomato. Beginning with the short end, carefully roll up the omelette. Slice into 1-inch pieces and serve with salsa.

Notes: The filled and rolled omelette can be kept warm for up to 1 hour before the final heating.

The Salsa Fresca makes a delicious, naturally low-fat accompaniment to egg dishes, grilled seafood and other brunch items.

Fabulous French Toast, Uncommon Pancakes and Waffles

These meals are designed to challenge the guest's expectations of what a morning meal might be. There are both sweet and savory dishes in this group, particularly great for entertaining or for offering menu options to those guests who are looking for an eggless morning meal. Many of these recipes may also be prepared the night before, then baked off just before serving.

In the spirit of making every calorie and fat gram pay for itself in enhancing flavor and taste, you will not find any of the usual side dishes here, which may seem particularly harsh to breakfast meat lovers everywhere. Nevertheless, I would no more imagine adding a piece of ham or scrapple to a special morning meal then I would entreat a waiter at a five-star restaurant to bring me a side of meatballs with an elegant pasta dish. But having lived with a bacon, ham and sausage lover of great devotion (who also is quite unfairly blessed with high metabolism and low cholesterol), I suggest you exert your own culinary creativity and freedom in adding the side dishes you desire.

Cinnamon Bread Pudding French Toast with Bourbon Sauce

Raspberry-Almond Croissant French Toast

Cornmeal-Crusted French Toast with Strawberry Butter

Walnut French Toast with Poached Pears and Stilton

French Toast with Praline Syrup

Cinnamon French Toast with Apricot-Cheese Filling

Blueberry Corncakes with Creamy Blueberry Topping

Lemon Cheese Cakes with Strawberry Glaze

Crisp Cinnamon Cakes with Maple Caramelized Apples

Minted Pancakes with Raspberry Coulis

Pancakes with Tangy Chutney

Chocolate Chip Pancakes with Cinnamon Bananas

Corn Waffles with Smoked Salmon and Caviar Cream

Walnut Buttermilk Pancakes with Sautéed Apple Rings

Belgian Waffles with Brandied Peaches and Blueberry Syrup

Pumpkin Waffles with Cider Syrup

Blackberry Crêpes with Blood Oranges and Mascarpone

Grilled Polenta Cakes with Cilantro and Sweet Corn Salsa

Nutmeg Risotto Cakes with Rum Raisin Syrup

Gingerbread Cakes with Apple Raisin Syrup

Cinnamon Bread Pudding French Toast with Bourbon Sauce

Bread Pudding

12 slices French bread, cubed
1 cup walnuts
2 cups milk
2 cups half-and-half
5 eggs
½ cup plus 3 tablespoons sugar
1 teaspoon vanilla extract
3 teaspoons cinnamon

Bourbon Sauce

1 cup heavy cream
1 cup milk
5 egg yolks
½ cup sugar
¼ cup bourbon

Assembly

3 eggs
½ cup half-and-half
1 tablespoon butter
1 tablespoon corn oil

SERVES 6

This French toast is made with slices of a cinnamon-scented bread pudding, and served with a creamy custard in lieu of syrup.

Pudding: Preheat oven to 350° F. Grease a 9 × 5-inch loaf pan and set aside. In a medium bowl, combine the bread cubes and walnuts. Combine the milk and half-and-half in a medium saucepan and heat until just ready to boil; remove from heat. In a medium metal bowl, whisk the eggs and ½ cup sugar together until light colored and frothy. Gradually whisk in the hot milk mixture. Stir in the vanilla and 2 teaspoons cinnamon. Spoon the cubed bread and walnuts into the loaf pan; pour the milk mixture over. Combine the remaining 1 teaspoon cinnamon and 3 tablespoons sugar and sprinkle over top. Bake the pudding for 60 minutes or until firm in the center. Cool, then refrigerate completely before slicing.

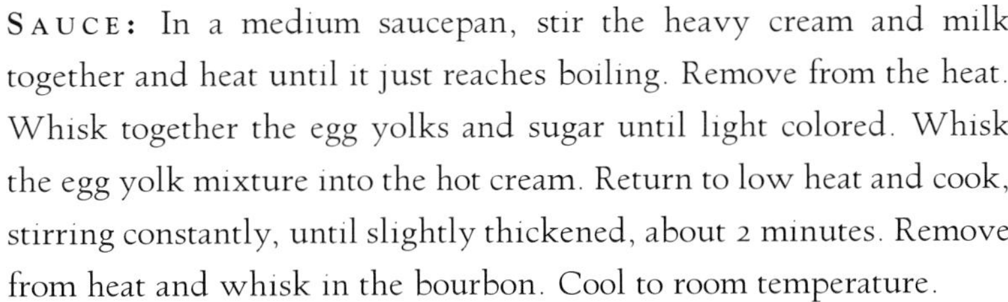

Sauce: In a medium saucepan, stir the heavy cream and milk together and heat until it just reaches boiling. Remove from the heat. Whisk together the egg yolks and sugar until light colored. Whisk the egg yolk mixture into the hot cream. Return to low heat and cook, stirring constantly, until slightly thickened, about 2 minutes. Remove from heat and whisk in the bourbon. Cool to room temperature.

Assembly: Slice the bread pudding into 12 pieces. Whisk together the eggs and half-and-half. In a large skillet, heat the butter and corn oil until the butter is melted and frothy. Dip each piece of bread pudding into the egg mixture, coating both sides. Cook slices in the skillet over medium heat until browned on both sides; keep finished slices warm in a low oven until all are cooked. Serve 2 to 3 slices on individual plates in a pool of custard sauce.

Notes: The custard sauce may be made up to 2 days in advance and stored in the refrigerator. The bread pudding is best prepared at least 24 hours in advance and may be made up to 2 days ahead.

Sautéed apple rings would make a delicious accompaniment to this dish.

Raspberry-Almond Croissant French Toast

Croissants

- *4 cups all-purpose flour*
- *2 packages active dry yeast*
- *¼ cup plus 1 teaspoon sugar*
- *⅓ cup warm water*
- *1 teaspoon salt*
- *2 teaspoons almond extract*
- *2½ cups milk*
- *½ cup butter, chilled*
- *½ cup mascarpone*
- *1 cup ricotta cheese*
- *¼ cup almond paste*
- *2 cups seedless raspberry preserves*
- *1 egg yolk*
- *2 tablespoons water*

Assembly

- *6 eggs*
- *½ cup heavy cream*
- *1 teaspoon almond extract*
- *¼ cup sliced almonds*
- *2 tablespoons corn oil*
- *2 tablespoons butter*
- *¼ cup mascarpone*
- *2 tablespoons amaretto*
- *¼ cup fresh raspberries*

SERVES 6

Our coastal inn in Maine was on the Bay of Fundy, where occasionally the thickest fog imaginable would roll in and blanket the town. Sometimes it lasted for days and was so thick that even the house across our small street was obscured. It was during one of these fogs that I perfected several versions of croissants and croissant dough. When we could not bear to taste one more croissant—hard to imagine but this was serious fog—this French toast made excellent use of the remaining dough.

Croissants: Place 1 cup flour in a bowl. Dissolve the yeast and ½ teaspoon sugar in the warm water to proof for 5 minutes. Stir the yeast mixture into the flour to form a soft dough, adding more warm water if necessary. Set the dough in a warm place for 30 minutes or until doubled in volume.

Mix the remaining flour with ¼ cup sugar, salt, almond extract and milk; add the risen dough and mix well. Cut the chilled butter into small pieces. Roll out the dough in a rectangle no more than about ⅛ inch thick and dot with butter. Fold the dough into three, letter-style. Turn the dough so that the folded edge is at your left, and roll out again; fold into thirds again. Chill for 30 minutes. Make two further turns, refrigerating the dough in between if necessary to prevent the butter from melting. Refrigerate until ready to assemble.

Preheat oven to 375° F. With an electric mixer, blend together the mascarpone and ricotta cheese. Divide the dough into 6 pieces. Roll out each piece to a 4 × 6-inch rectangle. Spread on the almond paste, raspberry preserves and cheese mixture. Fold the dough so the two ends meet in the center, forming the croissants. Pinch the ends together to seal in the filling. Whisk the egg yolk and water together and brush onto the croissants. Place croissants on an ungreased baking sheet and bake for 15 to 18 minutes or until light brown. Remove from oven and cool.

Assembly: Preheat oven to 375° F. Whisk together the eggs, heavy cream and almond extract. Dip the croissants into the egg mixture. Dip each croissant into the sliced almonds. Place the corn oil and butter in a large skillet over medium heat. When butter is melted and frothy, add the dipped croissants and sauté until lightly browned, 2 to 3 minutes. Turn once and brown on the other side, about 1 minute. Bake croissants for 5 minutes to heat through. Whisk together the mascarpone and amaretto; serve the hot French toast with the mascarpone and raspberries.

Notes: Frozen croissant dough, sometimes available at specialty shops, can be used. Defrost according to package directions.

The croissants may be made a day in advance.

Cornmeal-Crusted French Toast with Strawberry Butter

1½ cups hulled strawberries
1 tablespoon orange juice
½ cup confectioner's sugar
½ cup softened butter
1 cup cornmeal
3 eggs
1 cup buttermilk
3 tablespoons butter
3 tablespoons corn oil
12 slices brioche or challah bread
1 cup quartered and hulled strawberries for garnish

SERVES 6

A crunchy cornmeal coating along with sweet strawberry butter and fresh berries make this a delightful early summer treat.

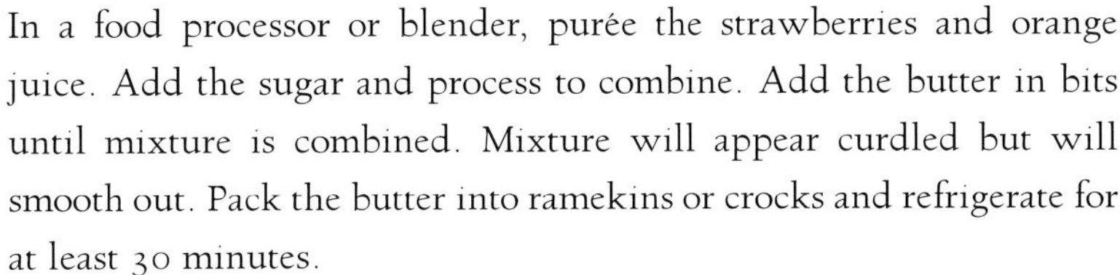

In a food processor or blender, purée the strawberries and orange juice. Add the sugar and process to combine. Add the butter in bits until mixture is combined. Mixture will appear curdled but will smooth out. Pack the butter into ramekins or crocks and refrigerate for at least 30 minutes.

Place the cornmeal in a shallow bowl. Whisk together the eggs and buttermilk. Heat the butter and oil in a large skillet until the butter is melted and foamy. Dip each slice of bread into the egg mixture, then into the cornmeal and cook over medium heat until lightly browned on both sides, 1½ to 2 minutes per side. Serve warm with the strawberry butter and fresh strawberries.

Note: This strawberry butter is delicious on toasted brioche and may be made several days in advance.

Walnut French Toast with Poached Pears and Stilton

3 tablespoons lemon juice
1 cup sugar
2 cups water
3 Bosc pears, peeled
6 2-inch slices of day-old French bread
¼ cup crumbled Stilton cheese
3 tablespoons cream cheese
3 eggs
¼ cup heavy cream
1 cup finely chopped toasted walnuts
2 tablespoons butter
2 tablespoons corn oil

SERVES 6

The combination of sweet and savory in this French toast will impress even your most sophisticated morning guests.

In a medium saucepan, combine the lemon juice, sugar and water. Bring the mixture to a boil and add the pears. Cook for about 15 minutes or until just tender. Remove the pan from heat and cool to room temperature. Remove pears from poaching liquid and cut into thin slices. Return poaching liquid to heat and reduce by one-half over medium-high heat until slightly thickened and syrupy, about 15 minutes; keep the syrup warm.

In the meantime, preheat oven to 375° F. Slice a 2-inch pocket into the top of each piece of the French bread. With an electric mixer, beat the Stilton and cream cheese until smooth and combined. Spoon a tablespoon of the cheese mixture into each pocket. Place 2 or 3 slices of pear into each pocket and return the remaining pear slices to the poaching syrup.

Whisk together the eggs and cream in a medium bowl. Dip each piece of bread into the egg mixture, coating both sides, then into the walnuts. Heat the butter and corn oil in a large skillet until butter is melted and foamy. Add the French toast and sauté each side over medium heat until brown, 1 to 2 minutes per side. Place on a lightly greased baking sheet and bake for 5 minutes, until warmed through. Serve warm with pears in syrup spooned over.

Notes: Poached pears may be stored in the refrigerator in the poaching liquid for up to 2 days.

The pear and cheese filling may be prepared up to 24 hours in advance and the French toast assembled the night before serving.

French Toast with Praline Syrup

Raisin Brioche

- ¼ cup milk
- 2 sticks butter
- ½ cup plus ½ teaspoon sugar
- 1 teaspoon salt
- ¼ cup warm water
- 1 package active dry yeast
- 6 eggs
- 5½ cups all-purpose flour
- ½ cup raisins
- 1 egg
- 2 teaspoons water

Syrup

- 1 cup orange juice
- ½ cup brown sugar
- 1 cup corn syrup
- 3 tablespoons butter, melted
- 3 teaspoons orange rind
- 2 teaspoons orange liqueur
- ¼ cup chopped pecans (optional)

Assembly

- 6 eggs
- ½ cup heavy cream
- 2 tablespoons orange liqueur
- 2 tablespoons butter
- 2 tablespoons corn oil
- 2 tablespoons cinnamon
- ¼ cup sugar

SERVES 6

Golden raisin brioche is easily made ahead as loaves and makes a wonderful starting point for an exceptional French toast. This recipe yields a bonus loaf for another day.

Brioche: Heat the milk and butter together in a medium saucepan until the butter is melted. Put ½ cup of the sugar and the salt in a medium mixing bowl; pour in the milk mixture and stir to dissolve and cool. Combine the remaining sugar and water; sprinkle the yeast onto the warm water; set aside for 2 minutes to soften and proof.

Stir the yeast mixture into the milk mixture. Add the eggs and mix until smooth. Turn the mixture into the bowl of an electric mixer equipped with a dough hook and add half the flour and all the raisins; mix until smooth. Add the remaining flour and continue mixing until the dough pulls away from sides of bowl, about 5 minutes.

Place the dough in a greased mixing bowl, cover and let rise in a warm spot until doubled, about 1½ hours. Punch the dough down and allow to rise again about 1 hour. Punch down and allow to rest for 5 minutes. Knead dough for 2 to 3 minutes, divide and form into 2 loaves. Place in 2 9 × 5-inch greased loaf pans, cover and allow to rise again until doubled, 1 to 2 hours.

Preheat oven to 375° F. Beat egg and water together and brush the mixture lightly over the loaves. Bake for 20 to 25 minutes. Cool slightly then remove from pans.

Syrup: In a saucepan, stir together all ingredients except pecans. Bring mixture to a boil, reduce heat and simmer for 15 minutes, or until of a syrupy consistency. Stir in pecans and keep warm.

Assembly: Preheat oven to 325° F. Cut the brioche loaves into 1- to 2-inch slices. Whisk together eggs, heavy cream and liqueur in a medium mixing bowl. Dip the bread slices into the mixture, coating them well. Melt the butter with the corn oil in a medium skillet. When the butter stops foaming, place the slices into the skillet and brown each side for 1 to 2 minutes; place the browned slices on a baking sheet. Combine the cinnamon and sugar and sprinkle over the slices. Bake for 5 minutes. Serve with warm orange praline syrup.

Cinnamon French Toast with Apricot-Cheese Filling

Cinnamon Bread

1 cup milk
¼ cup shortening
1 cup sugar
2 teaspoons salt
2 pkgs. active dry yeast
½ cup warm water (110 to 115° F)
6 cups sifted all-purpose flour
2 eggs, slightly beaten
1 tablespoon ground cinnamon
1 tablespoon soft butter

Filling

½ cup apricot preserves
3 tablespoons brandy
¾ cup ricotta cheese
¼ cup cream cheese
½ cup grated Monterey Jack cheese

Assembly

6 2-inch slices cinnamon bread
4 eggs
¾ cup cream
Dash of freshly grated nutmeg
1½ tablespoons corn oil
3½ tablespoons butter
2 tablespoons apricot preserves
4 apricots, peeled, pitted and sliced
¼ cup sugar
2 tablespoons brandy

SERVES 6

WE MAKE OUR OWN CINNAMON BREAD FOR THIS UNUSUAL French toast, but a well-made bakery bread would be a labor-saving substitute. The cheese filling is a wonderful blend of ricotta, Monterey Jack and cream cheeses. The apricot preserves add just a touch of sweetness to the creamy filling, which puffs as it bakes.

BREAD: Scald milk and stir in shortening, ½ cup sugar and salt. Cool to lukewarm. Sprinkle yeast on warm water in large bowl and stir to dissolve; allow to proof for 5 minutes. Stir in 3 cups flour, eggs and milk mixture. Beat with electric mixer at medium speed for 2 minutes. Using a dough hook, mix in the remaining flour a little at a time, until it makes a soft dough that leaves the sides of the bowl, or do this by hand. Knead with dough hook about 10 minutes or knead by hand on a lightly floured board for 12 minutes. Place in a lightly greased bowl, turning over to grease top. Cover and let rise in warm place until doubled, about 1½ hours.

Punch down, cover and let rise again until almost doubled, about 30 minutes. Turn onto board, divide in half and shape each half into a ball. Let rest 10 minutes.

Grease 2 9 × 5 × 3-inch loaf pans. Roll each ball of dough out into a 12 × 17 rectangle. Combine remaining ½ cup sugar and cinnamon and reserve 1 tablespoon. Sprinkle the mixture evenly over dough rectangles. Sprinkle with a few drops of cold water to smooth out mixture, using fingertips. Roll up like a jelly roll, starting at narrow end. Seal along edge and tuck ends under. Place, sealed edge down, into the pans. Cover and let rise until almost doubled, 45 to 60 minutes.

Brush tops of loaves with soft butter and sprinkle with the reserved sugar mixture. Bake in a moderate oven (375° F) for 35 to 40 minutes. Cover loaves with foil for the last 15 minutes to prevent excessive browning. Remove from pans and cool on wire racks. Makes 2 loaves.

FILLING: Mix ¼ cup apricot preserves with the brandy in a small pan. Heat to boiling point, then cool to room temperature. Mix together the ricotta, cream cheese and Monterey Jack cheese. Add the apricot preserves and mix well; set aside.

Assembly: Starting at the center of each piece, slice the bread through almost all the way to the bottom to form a pocket. Stuff the pockets with as much cheese filling as they will hold without oozing.

Preheat oven to 375° F. Mix the eggs, cream and nutmeg in a bowl. Heat oil and 1½ tablespoons butter in a large sauté pan. Dip the sandwiches into the egg mixture and sauté as many as will fit comfortably into the pan over medium heat, turning once, until golden brown on each side, 1 to 2 minutes. Place sandwiches on a cookie sheet. Heat apricot preserves to soften and brush over the top of each sandwich. Bake for 10 to 12 minutes or until the sandwiches puff and glaze.

Heat the remaining 2 tablespoons butter in a medium sauté pan. Combine the apricots and sugar and sauté for 2 to 3 minutes. Add the brandy and flame if desired. Spoon the apricots over the French toast and serve warm.

Notes: The recipe yields one extra loaf of bread, which may be kept in the freezer.

The French toast can be prepared the night before, so that the only A.M. work required will be the sautéing and baking.

The filling may be made up to 2 days ahead and refrigerated until ready to use. To save on calories and fat, skim milk ricotta and reduced-calorie cream cheese could be substituted.

Blueberry Corncakes with Creamy Blueberry Topping

1 cup all-purpose flour
¾ cup cornmeal
1 teaspoon baking powder
1 tablespoon sugar
½ teaspoon salt
1¼ cups low-fat milk
1¼ cups nonfat yogurt
2 tablespoons corn oil
4 egg whites
2 cups blueberries
¼ cup corn syrup
1 teaspoon vanilla extract

SERVES 6

Most pancake and waffle recipes use lots of butter, which packs a whopping 11 grams of fat and 100 calories per tablespoon. Ouch. While I firmly believe in balancing the downside of fat content with the desire for tasty foods, sometimes you just don't want to use up that fat allowance on one menu item. I find it's often difficult to convert an existing recipe into a low-fat version, partly because of the expectations established by the high-fat original that are difficult to match. I prefer to create original lower-fat recipes, so that the palate is challenged with a new taste, rather than rework something familiar. This recipe should satisfy a craving for pancakes without too much guilt.

In a large bowl, combine the flour, cornmeal, baking powder, sugar and salt. Stir in the low-fat milk and ¼ cup nonfat yogurt until combined. Stir in the corn oil. Whisk the egg whites to form stiff peaks; fold into batter. Fold 1 cup of blueberries into batter.

Heat a lightly greased griddle or skillet over medium-high heat and ladle on batter to form 3- to 4-inch cakes. Cook until small bubbles form and the edges begin to brown, 2 to 3 minutes. Turn and cook for 1 to 2 minutes longer, until just cooked through. Keep corncakes warm.

Whisk together the remaining 1 cup blueberries, 1 cup yogurt, corn syrup and vanilla. Spoon topping over warm corncakes.

Notes: Fresh fruit coulis (like the one described on page 110) also would make a delicious low-cal topping for these pancakes.

Lemon Cheese Cakes with Strawberry Glaze

Glaze

- *3 cups quartered and hulled strawberries*
- *¾ cup sugar*
- *2 teaspoons lemon juice*
- *1 teaspoon lemon zest*
- *1 teaspoon cornstarch*

Pancakes

- *1 cup all-purpose flour*
- *2 tablespoons sugar*
- *4 teaspoons baking powder*
- *½ teaspoon salt*
- *4 teaspoons lemon juice*
- *2 cups part skim milk ricotta cheese*
- *¼ cup corn oil*
- *6 eggs, separated*

SERVES 6

Light as an airy soufflé, these fluffy melt-in-your-mouth cakes are unlike any pancake you've ever had.

Glaze: Combine 2 cups strawberries, sugar, lemon juice, lemon zest and cornstarch in a small saucepan. Bring to a boil, then lower heat and simmer for 10 minutes, until slightly thickened and syrupy. Remove from heat, cool slightly and purée in a food processor or blender. Return to the saucepan and stir in remaining strawberries. Bring just to a boil and remove from heat. Keep warm.

Pancakes: Combine flour, sugar, baking powder and salt in the bowl of an electric mixer. Beat in the lemon juice and ricotta cheese until smooth. Beat in the corn oil and egg yolks until smooth. Whisk the egg whites to stiff peaks. Fold the egg whites into the batter.

Heat a lightly greased griddle or skillet over medium-high heat and ladle on batter to form 3- to 4-inch cakes. Cook until small bubbles form and the edges begin to brown, 2 to 3 minutes. Turn and cook for 1 to 2 minutes longer, until just cooked through. Repeat until 12 pancakes are completed. Spoon warm strawberry glaze over pancakes to serve.

Note: The strawberry glaze may be made up to 24 hours in advance and kept under refrigeration until ready to use.

Crisp Cinnamon Cakes with Maple Caramelized Apples

2 cups peeled and sliced apples
¼ cup maple syrup
3 tablespoons butter
1 cup sugar
1¼ cups all-purpose flour
1 teaspoon baking powder
½ teaspoon baking soda
¼ teaspoon salt
2 teaspoons cinnamon
1 egg
1¼ cups buttermilk
¼ cup butter, melted
½ cup corn oil, for cooking

SERVES 6

CINNAMON AND APPLES ARE COMBINED IN THIS DISH FOR a classic fall combination.

Toss the apples with the maple syrup. In a medium saucepan, melt the butter and add ¾ cup sugar. Stir until just combined. Add the apples and stir to coat. Cook over medium heat until the mixture thickens and just begins to turn brown. Remove from heat and allow to cool slightly.

In a large bowl, combine the flour, remaining ¼ cup sugar, baking powder, baking soda, salt and cinnamon. Whisk together the egg and buttermilk. Stir the buttermilk mixture into the dry ingredients. Stir in the melted butter.

Heat a thin layer of corn oil in a large skillet. Ladle the batter into the skillet to form 3-inch cakes. Cook until small bubbles form and the edges begin to brown. Turn and cook for 1 to 2 minutes longer, until just cooked through; lay the cakes out on paper towels and keep warm until all are cooked. Spoon apples on top and serve.

NOTE: Use 100 percent maple syrup for the best flavor. Our source for pure Pennsylvania maple syrup is Jacobson's Farm Syrup Company (RD #4; Box 690; Westfield, PA 16950; 814-628-5141), which accepts mail orders.

Minted Pancakes with Raspberry Coulis

- *2 cups fresh raspberries*
- *½ cup sugar*
- *3 tablespoons orange juice*
- *1 tablespoon framboise liqueur*
- *1¼ cups milk*
- *2 tablespoons sugar*
- *2 cups loosely packed fresh mint leaves*
- *1¼ cups all-purpose flour*
- *1 tablespoon baking powder*
- *½ teaspoon salt*
- *2 eggs*
- *2 tablespoons melted butter*
- *12 mint leaves and ¼ cup fresh raspberries*

SERVES 6

The flavor of fresh mint is infused into milk for this refreshing pancake—the perfect beginning to a warm summer day.

In a food processor or blender, process the raspberries, sugar, orange juice and framboise; set the coulis aside. In a medium saucepan, combine the milk and sugar and bring to a boil. Add the mint leaves and remove from heat. Cover to infuse for 10 minutes. Strain the milk, discard the mint leaves and cool to room temperature.

In a large mixing bowl, combine the flour, baking powder and salt. Whisk the eggs into the mint-flavored milk. Stir the egg-milk mixture into the dry ingredients until just combined; stir in the butter. Heat a lightly greased skillet or griddle over medium-high heat and ladle on the batter to form 2- to 3-inch cakes. Cook until small bubbles form and the edges begin to brown, 2 to 3 minutes. Turn and cook for 1 to 2 minutes longer, until just cooked through. Keep pancakes warm.

Heat the raspberry coulis in a small saucepan until just hot, about 2 minutes. Spoon raspberry coulis over pancakes and garnish with mint leaves and raspberries.

Note: The coulis may be made up to 24 hours in advance and kept under refrigeration until ready to use.

PANCAKES WITH TANGY CHUTNEY

CHUTNEY

- ¾ cup apple cider
- ¼ cup apple cider vinegar
- 3 tablespoons orange juice
- 1 tablespoon brown sugar
- ½ cup sugar
- ¼ teaspoon ground cloves
- 1 teaspoon cinnamon
- 1 teaspoon ground ginger
- 1½ cups peeled, coarsely chopped baking apples
- 1 teaspoon orange zest
- 1 cup cranberries

PANCAKES

- 3 tablespoons butter
- 1¼ cups all-purpose flour
- 1¼ teaspoon baking powder
- ½ teaspoon baking soda
- ½ teaspoon salt
- 1¼ cups half-and-half
- 5 eggs, separated
- 3 tablespoons butter, melted and slightly cooled
- 1 teaspoon almond extract

CUSTARD

- 1 cup heavy cream
- 3 egg yolks
- ¼ cup sugar
- 1 teaspoon vanilla extract

SERVES 6

THESE BAKED PANCAKES HAVE A LIGHTER TEXTURE THAN their griddle counterparts and a unique puddinglike topping. The chutney provides an unusual alternative to standard pancake toppings.

CHUTNEY: In a medium saucepan, combine the apple cider, cider vinegar, orange juice, brown sugar, and sugar and bring to a boil. Cook for about 10 minutes, until reduced and slightly syrupy. Add the cloves, cinnamon, ginger, apples, orange zest and cranberries. Cook, stirring occasionally, for 5 to 8 minutes more, or until the cranberries have "popped" and apples are cooked but not mushy. Remove from heat and cool slightly.

PANCAKES: Preheat oven to 415° F. Place ½ tablespoon butter in each of 6 4-inch ramekins or glass custard pans, and place on a baking sheet in the oven to melt. In a large bowl, combine the flour, baking powder, soda and salt. Whisk together the half-and-half and egg yolks. Whisk the egg whites until stiff. Stir the half-and-half mixture into the dry ingredients until just combined. Stir in the melted butter and almond extract. Fold in the egg whites until just combined.

Remove the custard pans from the oven and ladle the mixture into them. Bake for 12 to 15 minutes or until puffed and light brown.

CUSTARD: In the meantime, heat the cream in a medium saucepan until ready to come to a boil. Remove from the heat and whisk in the egg yolks, sugar and vanilla. Return to low heat until just thickened.

ASSEMBLY: Remove pancakes from oven and spoon on custard. Top with chutney and serve immediately.

NOTES: The chutney may be made up to 2 days ahead and stored in the refrigerator until ready to serve.

A single 8-inch round baking pan may be used instead of the individual pans. Increase the baking time to 20 to 25 minutes and cut the pancake into 6 wedges to serve.

For a seasonal change, try a topping of fresh strawberries or peaches with mascarpone cheese.

Chocolate Chip Pancakes with Cinnamon Bananas

Pancakes

- 1¼ cups all-purpose flour
- 2 tablespoons sugar
- 2 tablespoons brown sugar
- 1 tablespoon baking powder
- ½ teaspoon baking soda
- ½ teaspoon salt
- 1¼ cups milk
- 1 large egg
- 1 tablespoon corn oil
- ½ cup semi-sweet chocolate chips

Bananas

- 3 tablespoons butter
- ¼ cup sugar
- 2 teaspoons cinnamon
- 1 tablespoon brown sugar
- 3 ripe bananas, sliced lengthwise into 4 pieces
- 2 tablespoons brandy or cognac
- 1 tablespoon confectioner's sugar

SERVES 6

As sinfully addictive as Bananas Foster, these pancakes are sheer indulgence for chocolate lovers—imagine a white chocolate version with macadamia nuts and fresh raspberries.

Pancakes: In a large bowl, combine the flour, sugar, brown sugar, baking powder, baking soda and salt. Whisk together the milk and egg and stir into the dry ingredients. Stir in the corn oil and chocolate chips.

Heat a lightly greased griddle or skillet over medium-high heat and ladle on batter to form 3- to 4-inch cakes. Cook until small bubbles form and the edges begin to brown, 2 to 3 minutes. Turn and cook for 1 to 2 minutes longer, until just cooked through. Repeat until 12 cakes are completed; keep warm.

Bananas: Melt the butter in a large sauté pan. Mix the sugar, cinnamon and brown sugar together. Toss the bananas with the sugar. Add the bananas to the melted butter and cook over medium heat until the sugar begins to brown and caramelize, about 2 minutes. Add the brandy, ignite if desired, and cook until the mixture is slightly thickened, about 2 to 3 minutes. Remove from heat and spoon over warm pancakes. Sprinkle with confectioner's sugar and serve.

Corn Waffles with Smoked Salmon and Caviar Cream

1 cup all-purpose flour
1 cup cornmeal
1½ teaspoons baking powder
1 teaspoon baking soda
1 tablespoon sugar
½ teaspoon salt
2 eggs, separated
2 cups buttermilk
½ cup melted butter, cooled to room temperature
½ oz. caviar
1 cup crème fraîche
12 2-inch strips of thinly sliced smoked salmon

SERVES 6

THIS IS AN EXCEPTIONAL DISH FOR A MORNING MEAL that is equally at home as an elegant dinner appetizer. I use the finest Scottish smoked salmon and black sturgeon caviar for a beautiful presentation and refined taste.

Preheat a waffle iron. In a large bowl, sift together the flour, cornmeal, baking powder, baking soda, sugar and salt. Beat the egg whites until stiff. Whisk together the egg yolks and buttermilk. Stir the egg yolk mixture into the dry ingredients until just combined. Stir in the butter. Fold in the egg whites. Ladle the batter into the preheated and lightly greased waffle iron. Bake until light brown, according to manufacturer's instructions for doneness; keep the cooked waffles warm until 6 have been made.

Whisk together the caviar and crème fraîche. Divide the waffles among 6 individual plates and spoon on the caviar cream. Lay 2 strips of smoked salmon across the cream and serve warm.

FOLLOWING PAGES: *Corn Waffles with Smoked Salmon and Caviar Cream; Walnut Buttermilk Pancakes with Sautéed Apple Rings*

The
town

Walnut Buttermilk Pancakes with Sautéed Apple Rings

1½ cups all-purpose flour
2 tablespoons sugar
1 teaspoon baking powder
¾ teaspoon baking soda
½ teaspoon salt
½ cup finely ground walnuts
1½ cups buttermilk
1 large egg
¼ cup butter, melted and cooled
2 tablespoons butter
3 large cooking apples, cored and sliced into rings
3 tablespoons sugar
½ teaspoon cinnamon

SERVES 6

THIS IS PROBABLY MY MOST TRADITIONAL PANCAKE, juxtaposing the tang of buttermilk with the sweetness of fresh apple.

In a large bowl, combine the flour, sugar, baking powder, baking soda, salt and walnuts. Whisk together the buttermilk and egg. Stir the buttermilk mixture into the dry ingredients until just combined; stir in the melted butter. Heat a lightly greased skillet or griddle and ladle on pancake batter to form 2- to 3-inch cakes. Cook over medium-high heat until small bubbles form and the edges begin to brown, 2 to 3 minutes. Turn and cook for 1 to 2 minutes longer, until just cooked through. Keep pancakes warm and repeat until 12 cakes have been made.

Melt the butter in a large sauté pan. Add the apple rings and cook over medium heat for 1 minute. Combine the sugar and cinnamon and sprinkle onto apples. Turn apples and cook on the other side for 1 minute. Top pancakes with sautéed apples and serve warm.

Belgian Waffles with Brandied Peaches and Blueberry Syrup

Blueberry Syrup

- 2 *cups blueberries*
- ½ *cup sugar*
- ½ *cup water*
- 1 *slice lemon*
- ½ *cup light corn syrup*

Waffles

- 2 *cups sifted all-purpose flour*
- 4 *teaspoons baking powder*
- 1 *teaspoon salt*
- 2 *cups milk*
- 4 *eggs, separated*
- 1 *cup melted butter, cooled to room temperature*
- 1 *cup pecans, finely chopped*

Peaches

- 2 *cups peeled and sliced peaches*
- 1 *tablespoon lemon juice*
- ½ *cup sugar*
- 2 *tablespoons butter*
- ¼ *cup brandy*

SERVES 6

Peaches, peaches, peaches—the essence of summer's sweet taste. If you are not blessed with a local harvest of sweet peaches like ours, this preparation enhances lesser varieties with a fresh blueberry sauce. Use the sweet wild Maine berries, if they are available, or your own local ones.

Syrup: Simmer blueberries, sugar, water and lemon together until they form a syrup, about 10 minutes. Stir in the corn syrup and simmer 3 minutes more. Keep warm.

Waffles: Preheat a Belgian waffle iron. Sift together the flour, baking powder and salt. Combine the milk and egg yolks. Beat the egg whites until they form stiff peaks. Add the milk-egg mixture to the dry ingredients. Stir in the butter. Fold in eggs whites, leaving some peaks showing. Stir in the chopped pecans. Pour batter into waffle iron and bake according to manufacturer's directions for doneness. Continue until 6 waffles have been made. Keep waffles warm on baking racks in a low (250° F) oven.

Peaches: In a medium bowl, toss the peaches and lemon juice together to prevent browning. Stir in the sugar and set aside. Melt 2 tablespoons butter in a large sauté pan and sauté peaches over medium heat for 1 minute. Stir in brandy, and ignite or cook on low heat for 3 to 5 minutes. Remove from heat.

Assembly: Place waffles on individual plates. Spoon some peaches into the centers and serve with wild Maine blueberry syrup.

Note: The blueberry syrup may be made up to 2 days ahead, and refrigerated and reheated for serving.

Pumpkin Waffles with Cider Syrup

Syrup

- 2 cups apple cider
- 1 teaspoon cinnamon
- ¼ teaspoon ground cloves
- ¼ teaspoon freshly grated nutmeg
- 3 tablespoons orange juice
- ½ cup brown sugar
- ½ cup maple syrup
- ½ cup corn syrup
- 2 tablespoons butter

Waffles

- 2 cups all-purpose flour
- ¼ cup sugar
- 4 teaspoons baking powder
- 1 teaspoon salt
- 1 teaspoon cinnamon
- 1 teaspoon ginger
- ¼ teaspoon cloves
- 1½ cups milk
- 1 cup pumpkin purée, homemade (page 34) or canned
- 4 eggs, separated
- 1 cup butter, melted

Assembly

- ¼ cup heavy cream
- 1 cup mascarpone
- 2 tablespoons sugar

SERVES 6

Fall is a festive time in our area—the leaves display a spectacular array of colors and the farmstands are decorated with hay bales and Indian corn. Many feature fresh apple cider and huge piles of pumpkins in every size, some for carving and others perfect for baking these tender waffles.

Syrup: In a medium saucepan, combine the cider, cinnamon, cloves, nutmeg and orange juice and bring to a boil. Lower heat and simmer for 5 minutes. Stir in the brown sugar, maple syrup, corn syrup and butter and simmer uncovered for about 15 minutes longer, until slightly thickened and syrupy. Keep warm.

Waffles: Preheat the waffle iron. In a large bowl, combine the flour, sugar, baking powder, salt, cinnamon, ginger and cloves. Whisk together the milk, pumpkin purée and egg yolks. Stir the pumpkin mixture into the dry ingredients. Whisk the egg whites until stiff. Stir in the melted butter. Fold in the egg whites. Ladle batter onto the heated waffle iron and cook until lightly browned. Keep waffles warm until six are finished.

Assembly: Whip the heavy cream to soft peaks. Whisk together the mascarpone and sugar. Fold the whipped cream into the mascarpone. Serve each waffle with mascarpone cream and warm syrup.

Note: The cider syrup may be made up to 2 days in advance and refrigerated until ready to use.

Blackberry Crêpes with Blood Oranges and Mascarpone

1 cup mascarpone cheese
3 egg yolks
2 cups ricotta cheese
½ cup sugar
2 teaspoons grated orange zest
¼ cup blood orange juice
2 tablespoons orange brandy liqueur
¾ cup all-purpose flour
2 tablespoons sugar
1 egg
1 egg yolk
¾ cup half-and-half
¼ cup blackberries
3 tablespoons butter
18 blackberries, blood orange slices and 3 tablespoons mascarpone

SERVES 6

Blood oranges add a deep red color and unique orange flavor to these elegant crêpes.

With an electric mixer, beat the mascarpone until smooth. Add the egg yolks and beat until well combined. Stir in the ricotta, sugar, orange zest, orange juice and liqueur; set aside.

In a large bowl, combine the flour and sugar. In a smaller bowl, whisk together the egg, egg yolk and ¼ cup half-and-half. With a food processor or blender, process the remaining ½ cup half-and-half and blackberries until smooth. Strain to remove the blackberry seeds and pour into the egg mixture. Pour the egg and blackberry mixture into the dry ingredients and stir until just combined.

Lightly butter or grease a small crêpe or sauté pan. Heat the pan over medium-high heat and ladle in about 2 tablespoons of batter. Tilt the pan to evenly coat the bottom. Cook the crêpe through (but do not flip) until the edge begins to brown and curl slightly; slide the crêpe out of pan onto waxed paper or parchment; repeat until 6 crêpes have been made. Fill each crêpe with ⅓ to ½ cup of the cheese-orange filling on the browned side of the crêpe. Fold up sides of crêpe, overlapping filling, ending with seam side down.

Preheat oven to 400° F. Melt 1 tablespoon butter in a skillet over medium heat. Sauté 2 crêpes at a time on each side for 1 to 2 minutes, until golden brown. Repeat process until all crêpes are browned. Place browned crêpes on a lightly greased or buttered baking sheet and bake for 5 minutes. Top with fresh blackberries and mascarpone and garnish with the orange slices.

Notes: Filling may be made up to 24 hours in advance and refrigerated until ready to use. Unfilled crêpes may be made up to 24 hours in advance and stored in an airtight container.

Grilled Polenta Cakes with Cilantro and Sweet Corn Salsa

Corn Salsa

- *2 cups cooked fresh white corn kernels, refreshed in cold water and drained*
- *2 teaspoons chopped scallions*
- *½ cup seeded and chopped plum tomatoes*
- *1 teaspoon minced chile pepper*
- *2 teaspoons chopped fresh cilantro*

Cakes

- *2 cups milk*
- *1 cup water*
- *1 tablespoon butter*
- *1 teaspoon salt*
- *1 cup yellow cornmeal*
- *2 tablespoons mascarpone*
- *2 teaspoons chopped flat-leaf parsley*
- *2 teaspoons chopped fresh cilantro*
- *½ cup crème fraîche (optional)*
- *6 sprigs cilantro*

Serves 6

This dish, flavored with fresh sweet corn and plum tomatoes, incorporates the very essence of summer in the country. Try grilling the polenta cakes over charcoal for the ultimate summer taste.

Salsa: Combine ingredients in a small bowl. Refrigerate until ready to use.

Cakes: In a medium saucepan, combine the milk, water, butter and salt and bring to a boil over medium heat. Whisk in the cornmeal, a little at a time, until all is combined. Turn the heat to low and continue cooking for 10 minutes, stirring constantly. Remove from heat and stir in the mascarpone, parsley and cilantro.

Line 12 3-inch ramekins with parchment. Grease the liners well. Spoon the mixture into the ramekins and smooth the tops. Cover and refrigerate for at least 1½ hours, or until firm.

Assembly: Preheat the broiler. Unmold the cakes onto a baking sheet. Broil for 2 to 3 minutes, until just golden, then turn and broil the other sides. Serve the cakes with the salsa and garnish with crème fraîche and cilantro.

Notes: One 8½ × 4½-inch loaf pan can be used, which will yield slices rather than cakes. Cakes may be grilled over charcoal or on a gas grill if desired.

A great addition to this dish is chorizo, the fabulously spicy Spanish sausage that may be stirred into the polenta before molding.

Opposite: *Pumpkin Waffles with Cider Syrup; Grilled Polenta Cakes with Cilantro and Sweet Corn Salsa*

Nutmeg Risotto Cakes with Rum Raisin Syrup

Syrup

1 cup water
½ cup sugar
2 tablespoons brown sugar
2 tablespoons maple syrup
3 tablespoons dark rum
¼ cup raisins

Risotto Cakes

1 cup arborio rice
3 cups half-and-half
2 cups milk
2 tablespoons sugar
2 large egg yolks
2 teaspoons freshly grated nutmeg
2 tablespoons butter

SERVES 6

These are tasty little flourless pancakes with the flavor of rice pudding. Try them on a cold winter morning with the rum-scented syrup or in summer with some fresh berries. They may be formed the night before and sautéed just before serving.

Syrup: In a medium saucepan, combine water, sugar and brown sugar. Cook over medium heat, without stirring, until sugar dissolves. Stir in the maple syrup and rum. Simmer until slightly thickened, about 5 minutes. Stir in raisins, cook 1 minute longer and remove from heat. Reheat before serving.

Cakes: Combine the rice, half-and-half and milk in a large saucepan. Simmer over low heat for 30 minutes, stirring constantly. Add the 2 egg yolks and cook for 4 to 5 more minutes, until thickened. Stir in the nutmeg and cool slightly.

Form the mixture into 12 small cakes on lightly greased waxed paper. Heat the butter in a large skillet until melted and foamy. Add the risotto cakes and cook for 1 minute on each side over medium heat until lightly browned. Serve warm with the syrup.

Note: The syrup may be made up to 2 days in advance.

Gingerbread Cakes with Apple Raisin Syrup

Syrup

- *2 cups apple cider*
- *¼ cup sugar*
- *¼ cup brown sugar*
- *½ cup corn syrup*
- *¼ teaspoon ground cloves*
- *2 cups peeled and chopped apples*
- *¼ cup raisins*

Cakes

- *2 cups all-purpose flour*
- *2 tablespoons brown sugar*
- *2 teaspoons baking powder*
- *½ teaspoon salt*
- *1½ teaspoons ginger*
- *¼ teaspoon ground cloves*
- *½ teaspoon freshly grated nutmeg*
- *2 eggs*
- *¼ cup molasses*
- *1¼ cups buttermilk*
- *2 tablespoons corn oil*

SERVES 6

On the first crisp fall day, I bake my first of many pans of gingerbread to serve warm with tea. These little breakfast cakes will give you that same warm-all-over feeling without waiting all day.

Syrup: In a medium saucepan, combine the cider, sugar, brown sugar, corn syrup and cloves. Bring to a boil, then lower heat and simmer until slightly thickened and syrupy, about 15 minutes. Add the apples and raisins and cook 3 minutes more; keep warm.

Cakes: In a large bowl, combine the flour, brown sugar, baking powder, salt, ginger, cloves and nutmeg. In a separate bowl, beat the eggs, molasses and buttermilk until well combined. Stir the buttermilk mixture into the dry ingredients until just combined. Stir the corn oil into the batter.

Heat a lightly greased griddle or skillet over medium-high heat and ladle on batter to form 3- to 4-inch cakes. Cook until small bubbles form and the edges begin to brown, 2 to 3 minutes. Turn and cook for 1 to 2 minutes longer, until just cooked through. Continue until 12 cakes are completed. Divide among 6 plates and spoon syrup on to serve.

Late Risers—Buffets and Brunches

How wonderfully indulgent to sleep late, read the Sunday paper, perhaps with coffee in bed, and then rise midday to discover a fabulous buffet of exquisite tastes laid out before you. This is the fantasy that has come to be called "brunch," the best of the morning meal drifting languidly right into the afternoon.

While any of our menu items would be wonderfully at place for brunch, the choices in this chapter will round out your buffet menus or provide a substantial later meal.

Chicken Salad with Tarragon Pesto and Red Grapes

Soft Shell Crabs with Almonds and Shallot-Dill Vinaigrette

Crabcakes with Old Bay Potatoes and Dijon Aioli

Curried Shrimp Salad with Mango Peach Mayonnaise

Napoleon of Smoked Salmon, Goat Cheese and Dill

Scallops with Pink Grapefruit and Caviar

Marinated Tuna Carpaccio with Herb Vinaigrette

Mushroom, Fontina and Prosciutto Ravioli

Tortellini Salad with Gorgonzola, Roasted Peppers and Pepper-Oil

Baked Goat Cheese with Roasted Red Pepper and Mesclun

Phyllo Packets with Lobster, Gruyère and Tarragon

Smoked Salmon and Scallop Terrine with Dill, Lemon and Capers

Roasted Pork Tenderloin with Caramelized Apples and Mustard Sauce

Trout with Cornmeal Crust and White Wine Chive Sauce

Radicchio and Mushroom Salad with Balsamic Vinaigrette

Watercress and Frisée Salad with Roquefort and Warm Pancetta Dressing

Wild Rice and Almonds with Orange Vinaigrette

Duck and Spinach Salad with Raspberry Vinaigrette

Eggplant Strata with Caramelized Onions, Zucchini, and Fresh Tomato Sauce

Endive with Smoked Chicken and Gorgonzola Salad

Chicken Salad with Tarragon Pesto and Red Grapes

½ cup white wine
1 teaspoon salt
1 tablespoon peppercorns
1 small onion, peeled and halved
2 whole chicken breasts, about 3 lbs.
¾ cup mayonnaise, homemade (recipe follows) or store-bought
1 teaspoon Dijon mustard
3 tablespoons fresh Herb Pesto made with tarragon (page 66)
1 full bunch red seedless grapes (about 20 grapes)
½ cup pine nuts
2 cups tender lettuce and alfalfa sprouts for garnish

SERVES 6

The average chicken salad becomes extraordinary with the addition of fresh pesto. Many herb pestos could work, particularly basil or dill, but I generally use fresh tarragon with ours.

Fresh herbs from a windowsill garden will greatly enhance even the most basic dishes. A larger garden is great for variety and, in our case, volume. Because our land is so fertile, in the summer many of our herb plants resemble small trees with two-inch "trunks."

In a large saucepan combine the wine, salt, peppercorns and onion. Add the chicken breasts and just enough water to cover. Heat to a gentle boil. Simmer for 10 minutes on low heat or until the chicken is just cooked through. Remove from heat and allow to cool in the liquid.

Combine the mayonnaise, mustard and pesto. Remove the chicken from the bone, discard the skin and separate the meat by hand into small pieces; toss with the mayonnaise mixture. Add the grapes and pine nuts and serve on a bed of fresh greens and sprouts.

NOTE: Chicken salad may be made up to 1 day in advance.

Mayonnaise

1 egg yolk
¾ cup corn oil
1 tablespoon white vinegar
½ teaspoon salt

MAKES 3/4 CUP

Process the egg yolk until light-colored. Very gradually—drop by drop—add about ½ cup oil while continuously beating, to allow the mixture to emulsify and thicken. Add the rest of the oil in a slow, thin trickle until it is fully incorporated. Beat in the vinegar and salt. Cover and refrigerate immediately; the mayonnaise will keep for about 8 days.

NOTE: You can salvage a separated batch of mayonnaise by starting with a clean bowl and egg yolk, then adding the mixture slowly, as described above for the oil.

Soft Shell Crabs with Almonds and Shallot-Dill Vinaigrette

4 tablespoons chopped shallots
¼ cup chopped fresh dill
¼ cup corn oil
2 tablespoons extra-virgin olive oil
1 teaspoon lemon juice
1 teaspoon lemon zest
1 teaspoon white wine vinegar
6 soft-shell crabs, pan ready (ask the fishmonger to do this)
¼ cup all-purpose flour
1 teaspoon salt
1 teaspoon pepper
1 egg
1 tablespoon milk
½ cup sliced almonds
3 tablespoons clarified butter
1 cup fresh mesclun or other tender lettuce

SERVES 6

Fresh soft-shell crabs, also known as "peelers," are available from Chesapeake fishmongers in late spring. Almonds add a crisp outer texture to the tender crab within, which is eaten in its entirety. These are also delicious served plain or with Dijon Aioli (page 129).

In a food processor or blender, combine the shallots, dill, corn oil, olive oil, lemon juice, lemon zest and white wine vinegar just until blended; set aside.

Pat the crabs dry with paper towels, gently squeezing out any excess moisture. Combine the flour, salt and pepper in a shallow bowl. Whisk together the egg and milk in a second shallow bowl. Dredge each crab in the flour, then the egg, and finally the almonds. Heat the butter in a large skillet. Add the crabs and sauté over medium heat for 3 to 4 minutes on each side, until golden brown and cooked through. Divide the mesclun among 6 plates and place a crab on each. Spoon on the vinaigrette and serve warm.

Crabcakes with Old Bay Potatoes and Dijon Aioli

Dijon Aioli

1 large egg
1 cup corn oil
2 cloves garlic, minced
¼ cup Dijon mustard
¼ teaspoon cayenne pepper
2 tablespoons white wine vinegar

Crabcakes and Potatoes

¼ cup oil
1 egg
2 cups shredded boiled potatoes
5 tablespoons Old Bay Seasoning
1 lb. jumbo lump crabmeat, carefully picked over
1 large egg, slightly beaten
1 tablespoon chopped scallions
1 teaspoon Colman's dry mustard
1 teaspoon chopped flat-leaf parsley
1 dash Tabasco
¼ teaspoon cayenne pepper
1 cup sliced almonds
Flour for dredging
2 tablespoons clarified butter

Assembly

1 teaspoon white wine vinegar

SERVES 6

Our unique location in Lancaster County gives us daily access to deliveries of fresh seafood from the Chesapeake, and this means two of my favorite *fruits de mer:* blue crabs and blue-point oysters. Although Maryland crab is available from late spring in good weather, the price of jumbo crab bottoms out late in the summer and a crab feast at the inn is in order. These jumbo lump crabcakes have only one secret: they have no filler. In the beginning, I thought I needed a few breadcrumbs to tie them together, but later I gave in to a purist's dream: giant lumps of sweet crab, seasoned with Old Bay and sautéed delicately and lightly (or broiled on a rack), then served with creamy garlic-scented mustard sauce and crisp seasoned potatoes.

AIOLI: Process the egg in a food processor or blender until light-colored. With the machine running, slowly add corn oil in a very thin, steady stream, allowing time for the mixture to emulsify. Add the remaining ingredients and process to combine. Refrigerate.

CRABCAKES AND POTATOES: Preheat the oil to 350° F in a sauté pan or small deep fryer. In a medium bowl, whisk egg lightly. Add shredded potatoes and toss to combine. Form potatoes into 6 shallow nests and fry until light golden brown, about 2 to 3 minutes on each side. Drain on paper towels, sprinkle with 2 tablespoons of the Old Bay Seasoning and keep warm.

Gently combine the crabmeat, egg, scallions, remaining Old Bay Seasoning, mustard, parsley and Tabasco. Form 6 crabcakes about 1½ to 2 inches across and dredge in almonds, then lightly in the flour (handle these delicately to prevent the cakes from falling apart). Heat the butter in a large sauté pan and sauté the cakes over medium heat for about 2 minutes on each side, until lightly browned and heated through.

ASSEMBLY: Place the potato nests on 6 individual plates and sprinkle with the vinegar. Place a crabcake on each nest and serve with the Dijon Aioli.

Curried Shrimp Salad with Mango Peach Mayonnaise

- *1 lb. large shrimp, peeled and deveined*
- *1½ teaspoon curry powder*
- *1 tablespoon chopped fresh flat-leaf parsley*
- *1 fresh ripe mango, peeled, pitted and sliced*
- *½ cup peeled, pitted and sliced fresh peaches*
- *1 tablespoon lemon juice*
- *¾ cup mayonnaise, homemade (page 127) or store-bought*
- *2 cups red-leaf or other tender lettuce*
- *Sliced kiwi and pineapple for garnish*

SERVES 6

Although I'm not a big fan of curries (it's probably good there's *something* I don't like to eat), I love the natural taste combination of shrimp, curry spices, peaches and mango in this salad.

Poach the shrimp in boiling water until just cooked, 2 to 3 minutes; immediately submerge the shrimp in ice water to cool. Toss the cooled shrimp with 1 teaspoon of the curry powder and the parsley in a large bowl.

With a food processor or blender, purée the mango, peaches and lemon juice until smooth. Add the fruit purée to the mayonnaise and combine well. Stir in the remaining ½ teaspoon curry powder. Stir the mayonnaise into the shrimp and toss until evenly coated. Divide the greens among 6 plates and mound the shrimp salad on top. Garnish with the kiwi and pineapple and serve.

NAPOLEON OF SMOKED SALMON, GOAT CHEESE AND DILL

1½ cups white wine
2 tablespoons chopped shallots
2 cups heavy cream
1 egg
1 tablespoon water
1 sheet of puff pastry (page 72),
12 slices of smoked salmon
½ cup crumbled goat cheese
½ cup cold butter, cut into bits
2 tablespoons chopped fresh dill

SERVES 6

THIS DISH WAS ONCE DESCRIBED TO ME BY A GUEST AS "inspired." I hope your guests will feel the same about it.

In a medium saucepan, combine the white wine and shallots and bring to a boil; lower the heat and reduce to about ¼ cup. Using a slotted spoon, remove the shallots. Add the heavy cream and reduce by about one-third, until slightly thickened. Remove the pan from heat and keep warm.

Preheat oven to 375° F. Whisk together the egg and water. Cut the puff pastry into 6 2 × 4-inch rectangles and place them on a lightly greased baking sheet. Brush with the egg wash and bake for 12 to 15 minutes, until golden brown. Allow the rectangles to cool slightly, then cut each in half. Place 1 slice of smoked salmon on each rectangle, cover with the crumbled goat cheese and top with another slice of salmon. Top with the remaining puff pastry rectangles. Place the napoleons on a lightly greased baking sheet and bake for 8 to 10 minutes, until heated through.

Meanwhile, return the sauce to low heat and whisk in the butter bits until well incorporated. Remove from heat and stir in the dill. Spoon sauce onto individual plates and place a napoleon on top of each to serve.

NOTES: Using fresh or store-bought frozen puff pastry will reduce the preparation time for this dish.

The baked shells can be kept, at room temperature, wrapped in foil for up to two days.

Scallops with Pink Grapefruit and Caviar

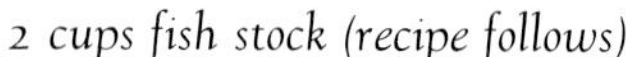

- 2 cups fish stock (recipe follows)
- 2 teaspoons minced shallots
- 2 tablespoons grapefruit juice
- 1 teaspoon lemon juice
- ½ teaspoon sugar
- ½ teaspoon white pepper
- ½ cup corn oil
- 5 tablespoons extra-virgin olive oil
- 18 jumbo sea scallops
- 18 slices pink grapefruit, skinned and seeded
- 1 tablespoon black caviar

SERVES 6

Sea scallops live in large flat shells. What we commonly refer to as a scallop is actually only the adductor muscle (the piece that opens and closes the shell).

In a small saucepan, combine the fish stock and shallots. Heat to a boil, then lower the heat and reduce to about ¼ cup. Cool slightly and remove the shallots. In a food processor or blender, combine the reduced stock, grapefruit juice, lemon juice, sugar and white pepper. With the machine still running, slowly add the corn oil and 3 tablespoons of the olive oil until well combined; set this vinaigrette aside.

In a large sauté pan, heat the remaining 2 tablespoons olive oil until very hot but not smoking. Add the sea scallops and cook until seared and just browned, about 3 minutes. Turn the scallops and sear for 1 minute. Add the grapefruit slices to the pan and sear each side for 30 seconds or until just warmed through. Remove the pan from heat and arrange 3 scallops and 3 grapefruit slices on 6 individual plates. Spoon on the vinaigrette. Top each scallop with a few grains of caviar and serve. This dish is equally delicious warm or cold.

Simple Fish Stock

- 2 lbs. fish trimmings from lean fish such as sea bass, red snapper, flounder or sole
- 1 cup sliced onion
- 2 leeks (green part only), washed
- 6 sprigs fresh parsley
- 2 sprigs fresh thyme, or 1 teaspoon dried thyme
- 1 cup dry white wine
- 4 cups cold water

MAKES 4 CUPS

Rinse the trimmings thoroughly and remove the pink gills from the fish heads if the fishmonger has not already done so. Break the frames into pieces. Combine the fish pieces and the remaining ingredients in a medium stock pot and bring the mixture to a boil. Reduce the heat to a simmer and cook for 30 minutes. Skim off the froth and strain the mixture through cheesecloth or a fine sieve. Cool and refrigerate if not using immediately. Stock may be stored in the refrigerator for up to 2 days or frozen in pint containers for future use.

Note: Avoid oily fish such as mackerel, bluefish, or salmon, which will give too strong a taste.

Opposite: *Scallops with Pink Grapefruit and Caviar*

Marinated Tuna Carpaccio with Herb Vinaigrette

Sashimi tuna is the high-quality fish used by Japanese sushi bars, and it makes a wonderful salad. For the marinade, I use a heavier—higher oil to vinegar ratio—mix than for the herbed vinaigrette, and a brief immersion time so as to not overtake the wonderful natural flavor of the fish. The vinaigrette is then drizzled on the greens only, since the tuna is already flavored.

Any tender leaf lettuce (Boston, arugula, etc.) would be delicious here.

Marinade/Dressing

- *¼ cup extra-virgin olive oil*
- *½ cup corn oil*
- *1 teaspoon minced garlic*
- *2 teaspoons chopped fresh parsley*
- *½ teaspoon chopped fresh basil*
- *2 teaspoons finely chopped shallots*
- *1 tablespoon lemon juice*
- *2 teaspoons lemon zest*
- *3 tablespoons cider vinegar*

Assembly

- *6 oz. sashimi-grade tuna, slightly frozen (see Note) and cut into paper-thin slices*
- *3 cups mesclun or other tender lettuce*
- *1 tablespoon capers, drained*
- *Fresh coarsely ground pepper to taste*

SERVES 6

Marinade/Dressing: Whisk together all marinade ingredients except the vinegar in a large bowl; remove and reserve half. Briefly dip each slice of tuna into the marinade and set aside. Whisk the vinegar into the reserved marinade to make the dressing. Toss the greens with the dressing and divide them among 6 plates. Top each plate with the tuna slices. Sprinkle with capers and freshly ground pepper and serve.

Notes: When using uncooked fish, always be sure that it is fresh and that you buy it from a reputable source.

The tuna also can be briefly seared before serving.

Freezing the tuna for 2 to 3 hours will enable you to cut paper-thin slices with a sharp knife.

Mushroom, Fontina and Prosciutto Ravioli

- *1 cup chicken or beef stock*
- *¼ cup red wine*
- *2 tablespoons minced shallots*
- *2 cups heavy cream*
- *1 teaspoon fresh finely chopped rosemary*
- *2 tablespoons tomato sauce, homemade (page 151) or top-quality store-bought*
- *3 tablespoons butter*
- *1 cup chopped chanterelles (or other wild mushrooms)*
- *¼ cup thinly sliced and chopped prosciutto*
- *½ cup coarsely grated fontina cheese*
- *12 wonton wrappers*
- *3 tablespoons chopped fresh tomato*

SERVES 6

Tender ravioli can be easily made with homemade pasta or sheets purchased at your favorite Italian market. This recipe uses time-saving wonton wrappers, which make a firm packet for buffet service and are now widely available at supermarkets as well as at Asian food markets.

In a medium saucepan, combine the stock, red wine and minced shallots. Reduce until only about 3 tablespoons of liquid remain. Using a slotted spoon, remove the shallots and add the cream. Turn the heat to medium, bring the mixture just to a low boil and reduce by about one-third, until slightly thickened, about 10 minutes. Stir in the rosemary and tomato sauce and keep warm.

Melt the butter in a medium sauté pan. Add the mushrooms and cook over medium heat until just tender. Add the prosciutto and cook 1 minute more. Remove from the heat and stir in the grated fontina cheese.

Take the wonton wrappers and cut 12 circles about 4 inches in diameter, using a round cookie cutter or a glass for a guide. Spoon ½ teaspoon of mushroom filling into each wrapper; fold the wrappers over the filling to make half-moons. Using a fork, press the edges tightly together.

In a large saucepan, bring 2 quarts of lightly salted water to a boil and poach ravioli for 1 to 2 minutes. Serve with the sauce and garnish with the chopped tomato.

Note: Uncooked wonton ravioli may be kept covered in the refrigerator for up to 24 hours before serving. The sauce is best made no longer than 1 hour before serving.

Tortellini Salad with Gorgonzola, Roasted Peppers and Pepper-Oil

- *1 lb. frozen gorgonzola or other cheese tortellini (mixed flavors and colors like spinach or tomato if possible)*
- *2 bell peppers (red, green, yellow or mixed), roasted and sliced into strips*
- *3 oz. gorgonzola cheese, crumbled*
- *2 teaspoons minced fresh basil*
- *2 teaspoons minced flat-leaf parsley*
- *¼ cup pepper-infused extra-virgin olive oil, available in specialty stores*
- *2 tablespoons balsamic vinegar*

SERVES 6

TORTELLINI IS LIKE AMBROSIA TO ME, FOOD OF THE GODS. Making fresh pasta is a wonderful experience in itself, and homemade tortellini is particularly satisfying. A good second choice is to have access to an Italian market where the pasta is freshly made.

Bring a large pot of salted water to a boil. Drop in the frozen tortellini and cook for about 8 minutes; test for doneness—they should be slightly firm and chewy. Drain and immediately rinse with cold water; cool to room temperature. Toss the tortellini with the peppers and sprinkle with the cheese. Whisk the basil and parsley into the pepper-olive oil and pour the mixture over tortellini; toss to coat and refrigerate. When ready to serve, sprinkle with the vinegar and toss again.

NOTE: To roast peppers:

Method One: Use a long fork to hold the peppers over an open flame or place them under a preheated broiler, turning them occasionally, until the skin is charred all over. Place the peppers in a paper bag, close tightly and set aside to steam for 15 minutes. Peel the skins off. This method is best for a small number and has the benefit of not needing the oven.

Method Two: This is the one I prefer since it requires less hands-on effort and is good for large numbers. Put the peppers in a preheated 475° F oven for 30 minutes or until the skins are charred. Steam and peel as above. Unused peppers can be stored in olive oil in the refrigerator for about 7 days.

Baked Goat Cheese with Roasted Red Pepper and Mesclun

6 oz. goat cheese
2 oz. cream cheese, softened
½ chopped roasted red pepper
1 tablespoon chopped flat-leaf parsley
½ cup fresh breadcrumbs
½ cup corn oil
2 tablespoons extra-virgin olive oil
1 tablespoon chopped shallots
2 teaspoons chopped fresh dill
2 tablespoons cider vinegar
2 cups mesclun, rinsed and dried

SERVES 6

Creamy goat cheese is combined with smooth roasted pepper for a delicious salad combination. A little cream cheese is added to soften the tang of the goat cheese.

Preheat oven to 375° F. In a large bowl or with an electric mixer, combine the goat cheese and softened cream cheese until smooth. Stir in ¼ cup chopped roasted pepper until just combined. Form 6 small round cakes from the cheese mixture. Combine the parsley and the breadcrumbs in a shallow bowl. Dip each goat cheese cake into the breadcrumb mixture. Place the cakes on a baking sheet and bake for 8 to 10 minutes, until warmed through and slightly soft.

In a food processor or blender, combine the corn oil, olive oil, shallots, dill and cider vinegar. Toss the mesclun with the vinaigrette and divide among 6 plates. Place a warm baked goat cheese cake on each plate and serve.

Notes: The tender quality of mesclun makes it especially perishable, so it's best to not rinse it until close to serving time.

Coach Farm makes a creamy fresh goat cheese with a tangy flavor unlike any from one of the larger commercial brands.

Phyllo Packets with Lobster, Gruyère and Tarragon

12 sheets of phyllo dough
½ cup plus 2 tablespoons clarified butter
2 tablespoons chopped scallions
2 cups fresh lobster, in chunks
2 tablespoons heavy cream
1 teaspoon chopped fresh tarragon
½ cup shredded Gruyère

SERVES 6 (24 PACKETS)

THIS FILLING IS A BLEND OF SUBTLY CONTRASTING TASTES and textures—chunks of fresh lobster, tangy cheese, and fresh tarragon—wrapped in a crisp packet.

Preheat oven to 375° F. If it is firm, melt 2 tablespoons of the clarified butter in a large sauté pan. Add the chopped scallions and cook over low heat for 1 minute. Add the lobster meat and cook until just heated through. Stir in the cream and remove the pan from heat. Stir in the tarragon and sprinkle on the cheese.

Melt the remaining ½ cup clarified butter. Uncover the phyllo dough and cut the sheets in half lengthwise. Brush one length with clarified butter and fold in half lengthwise. Brush this strip with melted butter and place 1 teaspoon of the lobster mixture at the end of the strip. Starting from the end with the filling, fold the strip as you would a flag to form a small triangular packet. Set the packet on a lightly greased baking sheet and cover with plastic. Repeat this process with the remaining ingredients.

Remove the plastic and brush the packets with any remaining butter. Bake for 18 to 20 minutes, until lightly browned and crisp.

NOTES: These make perfect hors d'oeuvres and can be made ahead and stored in the refrigerator, unbaked, for up to two days or for two weeks in the freezer. Bake for 20 to 25 minutes, until lightly browned and crisp.

Keep the phyllo dough covered with a slightly damp towel to prevent it from drying out. See note on page 36.

Smoked Salmon and Scallop Terrine with Dill, Lemon and Capers

Terrine

1 lb. sea scallops
3 egg whites
1 teaspoon salt
1 teaspoon white pepper
Pinch of cayenne pepper
2 tablespoons brandy (optional)
4 teaspoons chopped fresh dill
1 cup heavy cream
½ lb. smoked salmon pieces
½ cup fresh dill sprigs

Dill and Caper Sauce

1 cup crème fraîche
1 teaspoon chopped shallots
¼ cup chopped fresh dill
1 tablespoon lemon juice
1 tablespoon horseradish
3 tablespoons large capers, drained

Assembly

Fresh dill sprigs for garnish

SERVES 6 TO 8

THIS CREAMY COOL TERRINE IS A CINCH TO MAKE—ADD a fresh dill sauce and it becomes sheer elegance. Scallops have a natural viscosity that adds texture and body to this dish, and layering the scallop and salmon mixtures makes a stunning presentation.

TERRINE: Preheat oven to 350° F. In the bowl of a food processor or blender, process the scallops for 2 minutes. Add the egg whites, salt, pepper, cayenne, brandy and dill and process for 30 seconds. Transfer to a large bowl and whisk in the cream, a little at a time until the mixture is smooth.

In a food processor or blender, process the salmon and ½ of the scallop mixture until combined. You now have two bowls, one with scallops only (white), the other with salmon and scallops (pink).

Butter a 5-cup loaf pan or rectangular mold. Spread half the salmon mixture in the bottom. Lay ⅓ of the dill sprigs across the layer. Carefully spoon on half the scallop mixture; repeat the layers. Smooth the surface; cut a piece of waxed paper to fit the pan and lay it on the surface of the top layer. Cover the pan with foil. Set the pan in a 2½-inch-deep hot-water bath, place in the oven and bake for 1 hour. Remove the pan from the water bath, and cool to room temperature. Unmold the terrine and wrap it with plastic wrap. Refrigerate until chilled.

SAUCE: Whisk together the crème fraîche and shallots. Stir in ¼ cup dill, lemon juice, horseradish and capers.

ASSEMBLY: Cut the terrine into ½-inch-thick slices, arrange them on plates and spoon the sauce to the side; garnish with the fresh dill sprigs.

NOTE: The terrine may be made up to 2 days ahead.

CHATEAU

Roasted Pork Tenderloin with Caramelized Apples and Mustard Sauce

2 small (1- to 2-lb.) pork tenderloins

1 teaspoon pepper

½ teaspoon salt

½ teaspoon chopped fresh rosemary

2 tablespoons extra-virgin olive oil

¼ cup white wine

2 teaspoons Dijon mustard

3 tablespoons butter

1 cup sliced cooking apples

3 tablespoons brown sugar

SERVES 6

When I think of how the weather influences my food choices, I realize how much I enjoy living in a seasonal climate. Just describing this roasted pork dish makes me feel the cool, crisp air of autumn.

Preheat oven to 325° F. Season the pork on all sides with the pepper, salt and fresh rosemary. Heat the oil in a large skillet over high heat. Add the pork tenderloins and sear on both sides until just brown, about 2 minutes per side; place the seared tenderloins in a shallow roasting pan.

Remove the skillet from the heat to cool slightly. Return the skillet to medium heat and add the white wine, scraping the pan to loosen any meat bits. Cook for 1 to 2 minutes until slightly reduced. Whisk in the mustard and remove the skillet from heat; set aside.

Roast the pork until a meat thermometer registers 170° F, about 1 hour; remove the pork from the oven.

Melt the butter in a medium sauté pan. Add the apples and sprinkle on the brown sugar. Cook until the liquid is syrupy but the apples still firm, 3 to 4 minutes. Reheat the sauce, adding any juices from the roasting pan. Add the tenderloins to the skillet and cook briefly, just enough to coat with the sauce, about 1 minute per side. Slice the tenderloins diagonally into ¼-inch-thick pieces. Arrange on 6 individual plates and spoon warm apple on the side to serve.

Preceding pages: *Blueberry Bread; Roasted Pork Tenderloin with Caramelized Apples and Mustard Sauce; Trout with Cornmeal Crust and White Wine Chive Sauce; Radicchio and Mushroom Salad with Balsamic Vinaigrette; Wild Rice and Almonds with Orange Vinaigrette*

Trout with Cornmeal Crust and White Wine Chive Sauce

- *2 cups dry white wine*
- *2 tablespoons chopped shallots*
- *2 cups heavy cream*
- *1 cup all-purpose flour*
- *½ teaspoon salt*
- *¼ teaspoon cayenne pepper*
- *2 teaspoons chopped flat-leaf parsley*
- *1 teaspoon pepper*
- *2 eggs*
- *2 tablespoons milk*
- *1 cup cornmeal*
- *3 tablespoons clarified butter*
- *6 small trout, fileted, boned and skinned*
- *3 tablespoons butter, cut into bits*
- *2 tablespoons chopped fresh chives*
- *3 tablespoons chopped red pepper*

SERVES 6

THE FIRM MEATY TEXTURE OF TROUT STANDS UP WELL to the crisp cornmeal coating and becomes elegant with a creamy herb sauce. Wild rice with almonds is perfect on the side.

In a medium saucepan, combine the white wine and shallots and reduce to about ¼ cup. Remove the shallots with a slotted spoon and discard; stir in the cream. Bring the mixture just to a boil, then immediately lower the heat and reduce by half, until slightly thickened, about 8 to 10 minutes. Remove the saucepan from the heat and keep warm.

In a shallow bowl, mix together the flour, salt, cayenne pepper, parsley and pepper. Whisk the eggs and milk together in a second shallow bowl, and place the cornmeal in a third shallow bowl. Dredge each trout filet in the flour, then egg, then cornmeal. In a large skillet, heat the clarified butter. Add the trout filets and sauté over medium-high heat for 2 to 3 minutes on each side, until golden brown and cooked through. Whisk the butter bits into the warm white wine sauce over low heat until combined and stir in the chives. Place a trout filet on each plate and spoon the sauce over; sprinkle with chopped red pepper and serve.

Radicchio and Mushroom Salad with Balsamic Vinaigrette

Remember when radicchio was the fad lettuce of California cuisine? Perhaps it was the name that attracted some of the attention, but whatever the reason, we can all be thankful that it now is in daily use and no more a novelty. The crisp bite and beautiful deep red color of radicchio that has made it a staple in Italy for such a long time is the perfect counterpoint to the sweet, smooth flavor of fine balsamic vinegar.

¾ cup corn oil

5 tablespoons extra-virgin olive oil

1 teaspoon chopped shallots

3 teaspoons chopped flat-leaf parsley

¼ cup balsamic vinegar

2 cups radicchio leaves, broken into pieces

1 teaspoon minced garlic

1 cup sliced shiitake mushrooms

¼ cup toasted pine nuts

SERVES 6

In a food processor or blender, combine the corn oil, 3 tablespoons olive oil, shallots, parsley and vinegar. Divide the radicchio among 6 plates. In a medium sauté pan, heat the remaining 2 tablespoons olive oil. Add the garlic and sauté over low heat for 30 seconds. Add the mushrooms and cook over medium heat until soft and slightly browned, about 3 minutes; remove from the heat and stir in the pine nuts. Spoon the mushroom mixture to the side of the radicchio. Spoon the vinaigrette over the salad and serve.

Watercress and Frisée Salad with Roquefort and Warm Pancetta Dressing

- *6 slices of pancetta, chopped*
- *½ cup corn oil*
- *3 tablespoons white wine vinegar*
- *1 teaspoon minced garlic*
- *2 teaspoons chopped flat-leaf parsley*
- *2 cups watercress, stems removed*
- *2 cups frisée*
- *1 cup crumbled Roquefort*
- *2 tablespoons chopped toasted pecans*

SERVES 6

A SALAD OF TENDER WATERCRESS AND BITTER FRISÉE makes a delicious base for tangy Roquefort and a warm dressing flavored with Italian bacon.

In a large skillet, sauté the pancetta over medium heat until brown and crisp. Remove the pancetta and place in a medium bowl; set aside. Add the corn oil to the hot pan; immediately remove from heat and strain oil through cheesecloth. Add warm oil to the pancetta and whisk gently to combine. Whisk in the white wine vinegar, garlic, and parsley. Combine watercress and frisée in a large bowl. Spoon on the warm vinaigrette and toss to coat evenly with dressing. Divide greens among 6 plates. Sprinkle with the crumbled Roquefort and pecans and serve.

Wild Rice and Almonds with Orange Vinaigrette

2 cups cooked wild rice

¼ cup slivered almonds

¾ cup corn oil

3 tablespoons freshly squeezed orange juice with pulp, seeds removed

1 tablespoon cider vinegar

1 teaspoon chopped fresh ginger

24 segments of mandarin orange

SERVES 6

An easy and unusual rice salad flavored with fresh orange juice and almonds makes a versatile addition to a morning buffet.

Toss the wild rice and the almonds together in a medium bowl. In a food processor or blender, combine the corn oil, orange juice, cider vinegar and ginger and process until combined. Toss the rice and almonds with the vinaigrette. Arrange the mandarin oranges on 6 individual plates and spoon on the rice salad.

Note: Choose fresh ginger that is firm and juicy when sliced. Ginger is best peeled with a potato peeler or sharp paring knife. Peel only the amount you will use and store the unused ginger wrapped in plastic in the refrigerator. Unpeeled, ginger will keep about two weeks.

Duck and Spinach Salad with Raspberry Vinaigrette

Raspberry Vinaigrette

1 pint fresh raspberries
2 teaspoons sugar (optional)
1 cup corn oil
¼ cup raspberry vinegar

Assembly

2 8- to 10-oz. boneless duck breasts, roasted medium rare
3 cups fresh spinach (about 1 lb.), trimmed and rinsed well

SERVES 6

I ROAST THE DUCK BREASTS AHEAD AND CRISP THE SKIN under the broiler for an easy last-minute preparation.

DRESSING: In food processor or blender, purée ¾ pint of raspberries and sugar. Add the corn oil and vinegar and process to combine.

ASSEMBLY: Heat duck breasts briefly under the broiler to crisp skin. Arrange spinach on 6 chilled plates. Cut the duck breasts into slices about ½ inch thick, dividing each into 3 portions. Arrange the slices over the spinach. Divide the remaining raspberries among 6 plates and spoon the dressing over.

Eggplant Strata with Caramelized Onions, Zucchini and Fresh Tomato Sauce

- *2 lbs. eggplant, peeled and cut crosswise into ⅛-inch-thick slices*
- *1 cup all-purpose flour*
- *2 eggs, slightly beaten*
- *1 cup freshly grated breadcrumbs*
- *6 tablespoons extra-virgin olive oil*
- *¼ cup corn oil*
- *1 lb. zucchini, cut crosswise into ⅓-inch-thick slices*
- *2 tablespoons balsamic vinegar*
- *1 cup sliced sweet onions*
- *3 tablespoons marsala or red wine*
- *2 tablespoons balsamic vinegar*
- *1 pint Fresh Tomato Sauce (recipe follows)*
- *¾ cup freshly grated Parmesan cheese*
- *¼ cup grated mozzarella*

SERVES 6 TO 8

My mother's family is Italian, so growing up we enjoyed Italian food before it was trendy. Baked eggplant with Parmesan was served as a hot dish, but often the cold leftovers were pulled out for lunch the next day. I have an early memory of being told it was Veal Parmesan, and believing it—it was that wonderful a dish and still is. The quality of the cheese makes a great difference, and the Parmesan of choice is imported Reggiano. This version is made as a strata, or layered casserole, with the added taste of caramelized onions and zucchini.

Preheat oven to 350° F. Dredge each piece of eggplant in flour, then egg, then breadcrumbs. Heat 2 tablespoons of the olive oil and the corn oil in a large skillet and fry the eggplant over medium heat, a few slices at a time, until golden brown on each side. Drain the slices on paper towels. Clean the skillet and heat 2 tablespoons olive oil. Sauté the zucchini over medium heat in batches for 1 to 2 minutes each side. Return all the slices to the pan, stir in the vinegar and cook until absorbed. Remove the zucchini from the pan, add the remaining 2 tablespoons olive oil, and then the onions. Cook over medium heat for 1 to 2 minutes until translucent. Add the marsala and stir the onions until the wine is absorbed; set aside.

Lightly oil an 8-inch-square glass oven dish. Spoon in half of the tomato sauce then cover with layers of eggplant, Parmesan, zucchini, onions and the remaining sauce. Top with the grated mozzarella. Cover with aluminum foil and bake for 30 minutes.

Note: Dish may be assembled up to 24 hours in advance and stored covered in the refrigerator until ready to bake.

FRESH TOMATO SAUCE

3 tablespoons extra-virgin olive oil
2 garlic cloves, peeled and minced
2 lbs. ripe plum tomatoes, peeled, seeded and coarsely chopped
10 basil leaves

MAKES 8 PINTS

For sauce, the juicier the tomato, the more watery the sauce. I use plum tomatoes since they're meatier, and I squeeze out the seeds and water. If you use a food mill to process the cooked tomatoes, you do not need to peel them.

I make up tomato purée, which can be used to make sauce, at the end of the summer when tomatoes are at their prime and are least expensive. A half bushel—a large basket—of plum tomatoes yields about 8 pints of fresh purée. I simply chop the tomatoes into chunks, squeeze out the seeds and water, and then cook for 10 minutes, stirring frequently in the beginning to avoid sticking. Then I process the cooked tomatoes in the food mill. The purée is then substituted for fresh tomatoes in the recipe below.

My Italian grandmother canned her sauce in jars, probably because she did not grow up with refrigeration. I've found that freezing the purée in individual pint containers yields a fresher and most convenient flavor—frozen purée is better than using inferior tomatoes to make fresh sauce out of season. I also freeze some purée in ice-cube trays, then store the sauce cubes in freezer bags to use when only a few tablespoons are needed. I like my tomato sauce puréed, but if you prefer it coarse, omit that step. If you do purée and like a thicker sauce, return the sauce to the heat and reduce, uncovered, for about 15 minutes.

Heat the olive oil in a medium saucepan and lightly sauté the garlic. Add tomatoes all at once, cover and cook about 10 minutes. Purée the mixture in a food processor or through a food mill. Add fresh basil and serve.

NOTES: I am now going to help some of you to radically improve your cooking in one easy step. Proceed to your spice cabinet and remove and throw away any garlic products—minced, powdered, dried or otherwise artificial. Instead, always use only fresh garlic.

To peel a tomato, cut an "x" in the bottom and drop into boiling water for 30 seconds. The skin should peel right off.

Endive with Smoked Chicken and Gorgonzola Salad

1 egg
1 cup corn oil
1 cup crumbled gorgonzola cheese
¼ cup white wine vinegar
1½ cups diced smoked chicken breast
½ cup coarsely chopped walnuts
24 Belgian endive leaves (about 3 heads)
Alfalfa sprouts for garnish

SERVES 6

THE LEAVES OF BELGIAN ENDIVE MAKE AN ELEGANT BUFFET presentation and hold the perfect taster-sized portion of this dreamy chicken salad.

Process the egg in a food processor or blender until light-colored. With the machine still running, gradually add the corn oil until creamy and homogenized. Add ½ cup crumbled gorgonzola and the vinegar and blend until smooth.

In a medium bowl, toss the chicken with the dressing and ¼ cup walnuts. Place a mound of chicken salad on each of 6 plates and arrange 4 pieces of Belgian endive around it in a circular fashion. Divide the remaining ½ cup crumbled cheese and ¼ cup walnuts among the 6 plates and garnish with the sprouts.

NOTES: For buffet service or hors d'oeuvres, fill the endive leaves with chicken salad and arrange them on a serving platter or tray.

The salad may be made up to 2 days ahead.

Menus and Plan-Ahead Tips For Entertaining

These menus offer suggestions for combining individual recipes for special morning meals, whether simple yet leisurely breakfasts or festive brunch buffets. Each menu is followed by suggestions for dishes that may be prepared in advance. If you don't mind getting up rather early, these preparations can be done the day of serving, but to minimize morning stress, they can be spread over a few days. All items prepared in advance should be stored tightly wrapped and refrigerated as necessary.

In the same way that it's ideal to prepare most things right before serving, it's also beneficial if all your ingredients are fresh, but, again, in the real world, it's not always practical. I've lived in a remote coastal area in Maine, where our nearby store would

run out of mundane items like milk but lobster was always plentiful. When I lived in New York, inexpensive seasonal ingredients were not always available, but unusual ingredients could almost always be had, though at a price. I now live in an area where seasonal fresh produce is bounteous and inexpensive, but it is difficult to find unusual "gourmet" items. So the reality is that there are trade-offs in the realm of freshness. But there are a few things you can do to improve the quality of your morning meals if your resources are somewhat limited.

Here are my best tips:

- *Grow your own herbs. Through a local nursery or mail-order catalog, you can buy small herb plants that can be potted in a window garden for year-round use.*

- *Freeze ingredients at their prime. Since you know you may not be able to get good fresh strawberries in August, freeze some at their peak season in June. Good frozen ingredients are often better than soggy supermarket produce that was picked before its prime.*

- *Modify dishes, to make them not only seasonal but regional as well. Substituting locally obtained ingredients can often create new and interesting tastes that energize your meal. Then when your guests ask, "Where did you ever get this recipe?" you can confidently reply, "Oh it's something I thought up myself."*

Candlelight Bridal Breakfast

Festive Strawberry Breakfast

Sunrise Picnic

Garden Brunch Buffet

Harvest Celebration Breakfast

Leisurely Breakfast in Bed

Fireside Holiday Breakfast Buffet

Gala Celebration Brunch Buffet

Morning "Light"

Mother's Day Brunch

Hands-On Breakfast for Kids

Candlelight Bridal Breakfast

Creamy Arborio Rice Pudding with Amaretto and Caramelized Sugar

---

White Grape Juice Cocktail

Lemon Poached Pears with Berry Pear Sauce

Rolled Basil Soufflé with Roasted Red Pepper Coulis

Brides of all ages are enlivened with hope, the airy delirium that surrounds the anticipation of happiness today and forever, so designing a wedding event is particularly inspiring because of all the expectant joy of new love. Bridal parties are great for morning entertaining, since few faux pas can threaten the pleasure of a truly joyous day. This bridal breakfast is planned for early spring, when the countryside is tinged with shades of green, and fragrant narcissus and stately tulips break through the doldrums of late winter. Appropriately ribboned pots of hyacinths give off the scent of the season, and the sun gives welcome warmth through trees not yet in full leaf. This menu makes a wonderful bridal shower, a morning after the wedding send-off, or, enhanced by champagne, the wedding party itself.

TO DO AHEAD

Up to Two Days:

- *Make the rice pudding*
- *Poach the pears*
- *Roast the red peppers*
- *Arrange the table settings*
- *Make the party favors and placecards*

The Day Before:

- *Assemble the rolled soufflé*
- *Make the berry sauce*
- *Make the red pepper coulis*
- *Arrange ribbons on potted spring flowers*
- *Chill the champagne and beverages*

Festive Strawberry Breakfast

Strawberry Cream Puffs with Mascarpone
and Fresh Berry Coulis

Strawberry Pear Frothy

Strawberries, Bananas and Strawberry Mint Coulis

Strawberry Champagne Soup

French Toast with Strawberry Butter

The promise of summer is heralded by the first truly fresh fruit of the season—luscious red ripe strawberries freshly picked from the vine and delicately placed in woven baskets. In our country area, roadside stands seem to pop up everywhere in spring, with the juicy red harvest knowing no limits for weeks. When the strawberry harvest is at its peak, gather baskets of sweet delicious berries, then indulge with close friends in a casual springtime celebration that hints at the bountiful summer harvest to come.

TO DO AHEAD

Up to Two Days:

- *Make the Strawberry Butter*
- *Look for baskets or pottery for extra strawberries*
- *Arrange casual setting for guests*

The Day Before:

- *Make the cream puffs and store unfilled in an airtight container*
- *Make the Strawberry Pear Frothy and Strawberry Champagne Soup*
- *Dip the French toast in cornmeal and store covered in the refrigerator*

Sunrise Picnic

Hazelnut Cinnamon Biscotti

Lemon Poppy Seed Sandwiches
with Lemon Cream Filling

Strawberry Lemon Spritzer

Asparagus Egg Tart with Roquefort,
White Wine and Cracked Pepper

Late in the spring there is a brief pause, a moment when the midday sun provides a still pleasant warmth and when the cool evenings give way to perfect droplets of early morning dew glistening on each blade of tender grass. Spirit a special friend off to catch the sun's first rays on a quiet grassy meadow or to a pebbled beach to watch the sun climbing steadily above the blue-green ocean. In our Maine summers, this meant carrying extra sweaters and blankets, which were gradually peeled away as the sun rose and warmed the rocky coastal beach. Here in Amish country, we're likely to enjoy the peaceful early morning view of a farmer plowing his fields with a horse-drawn plow. Wherever you plan to enjoy your picnic, make it a morning to remember with a special quilted blanket to lie on or the scent of some freshly cut flowers in a festive wicker basket.

TO DO AHEAD

UP TO TWO DAYS:

- *Make the biscotti*
- *Make the lemon poppy seed loaf*
- *Pack the picnic basket with utensils, plates and glasses*

THE DAY BEFORE:

- *Make the Lemon Cream Filling and assemble the sandwiches*
- *Combine the strawberry and lemon juices for the spritzer*
- *Assemble the tart for baking (bake the night before and reheat if desired)*
- *Refrigerate the club soda*
- *Find extra blankets, pillows or tablecloths*

Garden Brunch Buffet

Peach Streusel Coffeecake

Blueberry Almond Tart with Frangipane

Orange Peach Iced Tea

Sweet Honeydew with Berries and Blueberry Banana Sauce

Cantaloupe Soup with Blackberry Swirl

Baked Tomato, Egg and Smoked Mozzarella in Phyllo Cups

Grilled Polenta Cakes with Cilantro and Sweet Corn Salsa

Minted Pancakes with Raspberry Coulis

Endive with Smoked Chicken and Gorgonzola Salad

Smoked Salmon and Scallop Terrine with Dill,
Lemon and Capers

Summer arrives on a warm evening breeze, with the smell of freshly cut grass and moments spent lingering outdoors past dusk tending a garden or simply savoring the longer days. The country is full of the scents and tastes of summer's bounty—sweet juicy peaches, berries and melons, just-picked herbs chopped and scattered on vegetables enjoyed within moments of harvesting. Summer flavors are immediate and acute—they require little enhancement—but they also are fleeting and best savored with immediate and full-fledged abandonment. Can anyone ever imagine in the deep of winter deriving such pleasure from a single food, the keen enjoyment that comes from consuming ear after ear of tender sweet corn or a plate full of freshly sliced tomatoes dressed only with deep-green basil? Summer's early hours provide perfect moments for entertaining, before intense heat and other distractions send us in all directions, even away from our very appetites. Plan for an outdoor setting, a balcony or a porch. Crowd the spot with potted plants and decorate with bundles of fresh herbs and fragrant nasturtium blossoms.

TO DO AHEAD

Up to Two Days:

- ☐ *Make the plain iced tea*
- ☐ *Make the chicken salad*
- ☐ *Make the terrine*
- ☐ *Arrange seating in the garden or on the porch and do last-minute cleanup*
- ☐ *Check for extra utensils, glasses and plates*

The Day Before:

- ☐ *Make the Blueberry Almond Tart*
- ☐ *Make the phyllo cups*
- ☐ *Make the Cantaloupe Soup*
- ☐ *Make the Orange Peach Iced Tea*
- ☐ *Make the Raspberry Coulis*
- ☐ *Fill the Belgian endive with chicken salad*
- ☐ *Make the Peach Streusel Coffeecake*
- ☐ *Lay out platters and serving pieces and arrange buffet table*

Harvest Celebration Breakfast

Carrot, Pumpkin and Pecan Cakes
with Orange Filling

Capuccino Hot Chocolate

Sliced Apple with Raisins, Walnuts
and Honey Poppy Seed Glaze

Pumpkin Waffles with Cider Syrup

No time is as keen to the senses in the country as the culmination of the season's labors in the final gathering known as harvest. Inherent in the idea of harvest is a joyous celebration, the rewards for the efforts of humanity and nature cooperating in achieving the common goal of survival. Harvest is a thread that binds us all together, the universal need to satiate ourselves today and the comfort of knowing that tomorrow our needs will be satisfied in what we've sowed and reaped. Early in the day we might gather together for a special morning meal and join hands in thanksgiving around a festive table graced with hand-carved pumpkins and fall flowers.

TO DO AHEAD

UP TO TWO DAYS:

- □ *Make the Honey Poppy Seed Glaze*
- □ *Make the cider syrup*
- □ *Plan breakfast settings and linens*
- □ *Carve pumpkins and look for colored leaves, mums and fall decor*

THE DAY BEFORE:

- □ *Make the Carrot, Pumpkin and Pecan Cakes*
- □ *Make the Orange Filling*
- □ *Make the hot chocolate*
- □ *Set tables and do final decorating*

Leisurely Breakfast in Bed

Raisin Scones with Lemon Curd

Cranberry Grapefruit Cocktail

Pineapple with Blackberry, Figs and Lemon

Cinnamon French Toast
with Apricot and Cheese Filling

The closest many of us ever get to breakfast in bed is room service, yet the very phrase evokes warm images of cozy comfort and pleasant surprise. Imagine the thrill of waking to enjoy this specially prepared meal, each item carefully laid out well in advance of the morning light, then perfected and brought to completion in the last waking moments. Freshly squeezed juice, succulent fruits and a warm-from-the-oven entrée—those special elements of a wonderful morning meal brought to bed on a tray, perhaps along with a fresh long-stemmed rose and the morning paper. Plump up some extra pillows and crawl in next to your surprised and no doubt elated partner, or enjoy this pleasure in blissful solitude.

TO DO AHEAD

UP TO TWO DAYS:

- *Make the French toast filling*
- *Make the Lemon Curd*
- *Make (or purchase) the cinnamon bread*
- *Locate a tray and linens for serving*

THE DAY BEFORE:

- *Make the scones*
- *Make the Cranberry Grapefruit Cocktail*
- *Assemble the French toast*
- *Arrange tray with place setting and fresh flowers*

Fireside Holiday Breakfast Buffet

Croissant Cinnamon Raisin Buns

Cranberry Apple Pecan Bread Pudding
with Vanilla Bean Custard

Cinnamon Nutmeg Eggnog

Orange, Kiwi and Banana Slices
with Orange Honey Glaze

Nested Eggs with Potato Blini,
Chive Cream and Caviar

Truffled Risotto Eggs with Spinach
and Shaved Parmesan

Walnut French Toast with Poached Pears and Stilton

The sights and sounds of the holidays offer such familiar joy—the gathering of family and friends in elegant apparel, the festive decor, the traditional holiday meals. Holiday traditions might be enlivened by a new option for entertaining—an elegant breakfast buffet served fireside in the peaceful morning hours. Plan the event as an informal gathering, perhaps served in the warmth of a country kitchen or in a casually arranged living room. A large grouping of candles might substitute for a fireplace; your family and friends will in any case be warmed by this respite from the bustling schedule of holiday entertaining.

TO DO AHEAD

Up to Two Days:

- *Make the croissant dough for cinnamon buns*
- *Make the bread pudding*
- *Poach the pears*
- *Complete holiday decor and plan table settings*
- *Check for serving pieces, utensils and buffet settings*

The Day Before:

- *Make the Vanilla Bean Custard*
- *Make Potato Blini*
- *Make Chive Cream*
- *Assemble the cinnamon buns*
- *Assemble the French toast*
- *Make the custard for the eggnog*
- *Make the Orange Honey Glaze*
- *Arrange and decorate the buffet table*

Gala Celebration Brunch Buffet

Apple Cheese Tart with Raisins and Walnuts

Raspberry Lemon Turnovers

Blackberry Cream Streusel Cake with Cinnamon Cream

Gazpacho Tomato Juice Cocktail

Wild Mushroom and Pancetta Soup

Eggs with Salmon in Dill Crêpes

Grilled Portobello Mushrooms with Basil Egg Topping

Cinnamon Bread Pudding French Toast with Bourbon Sauce

Pancakes with Tangy Chutney

Scallops with Pink Grapefruit and Caviar

Phyllo Packets with Lobster, Gruyère and Tarragon

Sometimes in entertaining you need to pull out all the stops. Often this occurs when the sheer joy of an event—a significant wedding anniversary, a career promotion or perhaps the birth of a child—warrants an extraordinary celebration. Sometimes these events are unplanned, so that part of enjoying their special nature is to seize the spontaneity of the moment. Other events, like the ushering in of the new year, have been celebrated so long in the same fashion that they might benefit from a fresh approach.

TO DO AHEAD

Up to Two Days:

- *Make the Apple Cheese Tart*
- *Make the bread pudding for the French toast*
- *Make the Apple Cranberry Chutney*
- *Make the Bourbon Sauce for the French toast*
- *Prepare the phyllo packets*
- *Arrange for decorations like flowers, balloons, streamers, etc.*
- *Check for buffet service and serving pieces*
- *Plan for additional seating as needed*

The Day Before:

- *Make the Raspberry Lemon Turnovers*
- *Make the Blackberry Cream Streusel Cake*
- *Prepare the ingredients for the Gazpacho Tomato Juice Cocktail*
- *Make the Wild Mushroom and Pancetta Soup*
- *Assemble the French toast*
- *Make the dill crêpes and the smoked salmon sauce*
- *Set the buffet table and chill champagne if desired*

Morning "Light"

Baked Apple with Oatmeal, Cinnamon
and Pecans in Phyllo

Strawberry Pear Frothy

Cantaloupe with Blackberry Peach Purée

Smoked Trout Frittata

It might be early spring, when the advent of warm weather reminds us that summer is close behind. The winter's cocooning has left everyone in need of a refreshing change of diet. The longer days encourage us to be active once again, digging in the garden or heading off on an early morning jog. Perhaps your breakfast is part of a weekend house party—you'd like to offer your guests a special morning meal, but one that won't overwhelm them the morning after an elaborate dinner party. Whatever the motivation, sometimes breakfast necessitates a lighter, healthier touch, with menu choices that are lower in fat. Fear not, food lovers everywhere, since lowering the fat in this case doesn't mean compromising taste. These lower-fat recipes will please the palate and honor a commitment to renewed health or will merely offer a deliciously light A.M. meal. With a little preplanning, there will still be time for an early bike ride or a brisk walk in the fresh air—but you and your guests will want to hurry back to enjoy these delightful breakfast treats.

TO DO AHEAD

UP TO TWO DAYS:

- *Make the filling for the apples*
- *Make the potatoes for the frittata*

THE DAY BEFORE:

- *Make the Strawberry Pear Frothy*
- *Make the Blackberry Peach Purée*
- *Arrange an informal table setting and seating*

Mother's Day Brunch

Almond Pear Tart with Apricot Glaze

Apple, Walnut and Raisin Strudel with Honey Glaze

Strawberry Lemon Spritzer

Wild Rice and Scallion Egg Tarts in Herb Crust

Lemon Cheese Cakes with Strawberry Glaze

Radicchio Mushroom Salad with Balsamic Vinaigrette

Trout with Cornmeal Crust and White Wine Chive Sauce

Remember the time you may have spent preparing a surprise treat for your mom on Mother's Day? Perhaps it was a special breakfast you prepared so that mom wouldn't have to rise from bed too early. Now you may have many "moms" to think of on Mother's Day—in-laws, grandmothers, stepmothers, or even someone who is "just like a mom" in how she's cared for you. You may be tempted to join the crowds of people who spend Mother's Day at a restaurant buffet. Instead, why not surprise your friends and family with an invitation to celebrate in the intimacy of your home, festively adorned with spring orchids or fragrant arrays of forsythia. One of the nicest ways to say thanks for any good deed is to celebrate with a special meal, and this elegant Mother's Day Brunch will suit the occasion perfectly.

TO DO AHEAD

UP TO TWO DAYS:

- □ *Make the wild rice for the egg tart*
- □ *Plan table settings and seating, check for serving pieces*

THE DAY BEFORE:

- □ *Make the Almond Pear Tart*
- □ *Make the Apple, Walnut and Raisin Strudel without glaze*
- □ *Make the glaze for the strudel*
- □ *Combine the strawberry and lemon juices for the spritzer*
- □ *Make the Strawberry Glaze*
- □ *Make the vinaigrette for the salad*
- □ *Make the reduction for the White Wine Chive Sauce*
- □ *Bake the crust for the egg tart*
- □ *Arrange forsythia, orchids or other flowers*
- □ *Set up the buffet table*

Hands-on Breakfast for Kids

Blueberry Peach Cobbler with Cinnamon Sugar

Cinnamon Peach Nectar

Sweet Honeydew with Berries and Blueberry Banana Sauce

Chocolate Chip Pancakes with Cinnamon Bananas